THIS BOOK IS FOR YOU

- you want to use the ideas to think for yourself and renew your

- you want not just to learn, but to learn how to learn, life long

The social reality around us is a pattern we ourselves have constructed. It is less fact and solid foundation than conjecture. Capitalism especially is what different cultures conceive it to mean. It is not "freedom" assured by some divine, global mechanism but a set of suppositions and rules we have constructed for better or for worse which should enter into dialogue with one another to find better solutions. A current crisis in this capitalism, similar to Brexit, gives us a chance to reconceive. We need to ask what an economy is for, and this means being "radical", less in the sense of socialism, than in going to the roots (radix) of what it means to create wealth. We need a moral science of economic development around which whole nations and regions can cohere.

This book tunnels down to our deepest and most basic assumptions and asks if these are not overdue for revision. Could thinking in a different way make work a form of self-fulfilment? To innovate is among the purest pleasures known to man. Can an entire culture find purpose and direction in what it supplies and consumes? One of the surprises in this book is just how many corporations and new movements have found that higher goals of human betterment are not only possible but morale-boosting and profitable to pursue. Profit is a needed fuel, not a destination, a means of expanding what you do, not an aim in itself. Economists may be right, money is at any one moment of time, scarce. But over periods of time, ideas are NOT scarce and the more of these you, have the more you can generate. And these turn from insubstantial mental constructs into valuable and substantial products and services. This book is dedicated to multiple ideas and harvesting these in lives lived to the hilt.

WHAT PEOPLE ARE SAYING ABOUT THE WORK OF THESE AUTHORS

TOM PETERS

"This is a masterpiece…." (comment on Riding the Waves of Culture)

WILL HUTTON

"An invaluable and path-breaking overview of capitalism's many hues." The Guardian (review of The Seven Cultures of Capitalism).

VINCE CABLE

"This is a major piece of work and is strongly recommended to anyone trying to understand contemporary business…" (comment on The Seven Cultures…)

CHARLES HANDY

"Authoritative, insightful and stimulating…" (comment on The Seven Cultures)

WARREN BENNIS

"Illuminates the darkness around the elusive concept of "culture" with a rich theoretical texture, and with powerful illustrations." (comment on Building Cross Cultural Competence)

PETER SENGE

"Profound, engaging, important, a wealth of illustration. A memorable contribution to systems dynamics." (comment on Corporate Culture: Vicious and Virtuous Circles)

MARSHALL GOLDSMITH

"Fons Trompenaars is a world authority on cross-cultural innovation..." (comment on Riding the Whirlwind)

MIHALY CSIKSZENTMIHALYI

"...A brilliant study that could benefit anyone responsible for the management of international high tech teams and those interested in group creativity." (Comment on The Titans of Saturn)

JOHN NAISBITT

"An important and brilliant book. With deep insights into China." (comment on Nine cultures of Capitalism)

R EDWARD FREEMAN

"It is a pleasure to read a book by two thinkers who actually understand how business works." (comment on Nine Cultures of Capitalism)

DOUG RAUCH

"the chapter on Conscious Capitalism is worth the price of the book alone." (comment on Nine Cultures...)

EDWARD DE BONO

"An intriguing book which explores the habits and methods of thinking across a wide range of cultures. It emphasises once again that traditional Western thinking is only one set of habits." (comment on Mastering the Infinite Game)

SIR PETER PARKER

"A necessary revelation….a fine piece of radicalism, beyond left and right, reconciling heaven and hell. In fact I keep thinking of William Blake's line "Opposition is true friendship." (Comment on Mastering the Infinite Game)

ROBERT F BALES

"An eye-opener for me …this book is so circumstantial, so concrete, co comprehensive, so well-presented ….that I felt I had known almost nothing about this subject before."   (comment on Mastering the Infinite Game)

GREGORY BATESON

"Much of it is very good….and some of it is brilliant." (comment on Sane Asylum: Inside the Delancey Street Foundation)

ABRAHAM MASLOW

"This is a brilliant and creative man. I was very much impressed." (comment on Radical Man: the process of psycho-social development)

SILVAN S TOMKINS

"A fine and passionate work…"   (comment on Radical Man)

MILTON KOTLER

"For the first time we have a brilliant psychological theory in support of self-determined community institutions." (Comment on From Poverty to Dignity)

About the Authors

Professor Charles Hampden-Turner has a doctorate from the Harvard Business School and graduated from Trinity College, Cambridge and worked in the USA for 21 years. He was Senior Research Associate at the Judge Business School at Cambridge University for eighteen years. He is author of Maps of the Mind New York: Macmillan, a Book of the Month Club selection. He was Goh Tjoe Kok Distinguished Visiting Professor to Nanyang Technological University in Singapore 2002-2003 and Hutchinson Visiting Scholar to China in 2004. He is a past winner of the Douglas McGregor Memorial Award and was the Royal Dutch Shell Senior Research Fellow at the London Business School. In 1984 he co-founded Trompenaars Hampden-Turner, the cross-cultural consulting company with his partner Fons. He is the author of twenty-two books, eight with Fons. Their books have been translated into twenty languages. Charles has won Guggenheim and Rockefeller Fellowships.

Professor Fons Trompenaars is an organizational theorist, management consultant and best-selling author, well-known for his seven-dimensional model of national business cultures. Riding the Waves of Culture (written with Hampden-Turner) has sold one third of a million copies. He was awarded the International Professional Practice Area Research Award by the American Society for Training and Development. In 2011 HR Magazine voted him among the world's 20 top international thinkers. He has been elected to the Thinkers50 Hall of Fame for management scholars. He is a professor at the Free University of Amsterdam and where he heads a course on Servant Leadership. He was until recently a partner at KPMG in Amstelveen. His latest book is 100+ Management Models which has won a prize in Malaysia. Until recently he had a column in the Dutch language edition of the Financial Times which described him as "a new star in of the world's management seminar circuit."

Professor Linda O'Riordan is a reflective practitioner with a doctorate from the University of Bradford in the UK. Her research interest lies in stakeholder management and responsible entrepreneurship focusing on sustainable approaches for business in society. Her academic activities include lecturing on Business Studies and International Management at leading Universities, and she is the Director of a Research Competence Centre for Corporate Social Responsibility at the FOM University of Applied Sciences in Germany. Her work has appeared in internationally renowned research publications and she is the author, editor, and reviewer of various academic books and peer-reviewed journals. Her latest highly acclaimed book is Managing Sustainable Stakeholder Relationships: Corporate Approaches to Responsible Management. Before becoming an academic, she gained business and consultancy experience from working in industry. Some of her former employers include Accenture, UCB-Schwarz Pharma, and the Government of Ireland (Irish Food Board/Bord Bia).

ACKNOWLEDGEMENTS

Acknowledgements always make us feel humble and wonder whether it would not be fairer to attribute "our" work to whole networks of people. It reminds us that independence is often an illusion. We are interdependent and have just one end of scores of relationships, through which knowledge flows. The first-named author owes most to his partner Fons Trompenaars, who has run our consultancy since 1984 and paid him from its proceeds. CMH-T cannot organize a proverbial paper bag. We are also grateful to Phyllis Stewart, the one person who knows on what plane Trompenaars, is currently flying and how and when to locate him. She is our sheet-anchor. Barbara Blokpoel collected, organized, edited, filed and commissioned many of the pictures in this book. Whenever CMH-T got lost in the Netherlands, she would magically appear amidst dense crowds to rescue him.

Talking of pictures, we owe much to the genius of David Lewis. We hope this book brings him the fame he so much deserves. While we think up the pictures and their messages, his wicked sense of humour saves us from solemnity and we often reflect that the joke may be partly on us. He spent hours drawing at the Royal Society for the Arts and his artwork drew interested spectators. CMH-T owes to Robert Eddison, his room-mate at Trinity College at Cambridge, an introduction to Chris Day, the Managing Director of Filament Publishing, who instantly saw what was intended in this book. We are flattered by his personal intervention as to how it should be presented and to his optimism about its prospects. We also owe much to the forbearance and patience of Olivia Eisinger, our editor. We are not masters of detail and we change our minds too often. If this book approaches coherence, thank her.

The kind words of trusted friends and fellow authors mean much to us. Among these are Charles Handy, Henry Mintzberg, Nancy Adler, Alan Barrel, Edward R Freeman, Clayton Christensen, Mimi Silbert, Peter Hiscocks, Ed Schein, Napier Collyns, John Cleese, Milton Bennett, Ida Castiglioni,

John Naisbitt, Vincent Cable, Tom Cummings, Hermann Simon, Raymond Madden, Tom Peters, Arie de Geus, Martin Gillo, David K Hurst, Ray Abelin, Peter Woolliams, Jay Ogilvy, Wendy Smith, Linda Putman, Edward de Bono, Marianne Lewis, Sylvia van de Bunt, Pi-Shen Seet, Cheenu Srinivasan and Raymond Madden. Many of those who influenced us most are now dead and we have tried to bring them briefly to life again in what we write, so their influence survives. These include, in the order of their influence, Gregory Bateson, Abraham Maslow, Rollo May, James McGregor Burns, Douglas McGregor, Chris Argyris, Donald Schon, Warren Bennis, Nevitt Sanford, Fritz Roethlisberger, Elliott Jacques, Carl Rogers, Adam Curle, John S Seeley, Richard Farson, John Maher, Silvan Tompkins, Sir Peter Parker, James Mitchell, Robert F Bales, George C Lodge, John Stopford and Tan Teng-Kee.

We owe much to three institutions, The Big Innovation Centre whose ideas we originally researched for this book and the Institute for Leadership and Management which has supported our work. Prof. Birgitte Andersen, Head of BIC, shared her ideas with us and enthused over our work in general, as did Niki Iliadis, Innovative Policy and Foresight manager. If female empowerment is to be like this, we look forward to it. Some of the better ideas in this book could be triggered by the BIC but the authors are entirely to blame for the remainder. The Institute for Leadership and Management has supported a much more comprehensive encyclopaedia of leadership published later this year, from which this book draws. We are indebted to Kate Cooper, Phil James, John Galvin and Beverly Hogg among others for their support and we hope these books will help them. The Institute for Manufacturing at Cambridge University and its annexe for pensioners has allowed CMH-T to stay in touch with contemporary scholarship and he is especially indebted to Yongjiang Shi, Chander Velu and Tim Minshall.

Finally we give thanks to our families, to Shelley Hampden-Turner and our sons Michael and Hanbury, to Penelope, our grand-daughter, who sketched the picture of the Unicorn company and Charlie. Let them all last longer than this book!

The senior author would like to give thanks to his family who put up with his preoccupation.

JOIN IN THE CONVERSATION!

Our mentor, Gregory Bateson, used to say that there was no form of communication superior to a conversation, preferably face to face, but otherwise by Skype or on-line. In conversations you can tell the other that the very question is mistaken, that the premise is wrong. You can re-define the whole topic. In inquiries claiming to be scientific, like questionnaires, you are often trapped in the mistaken alternatives of the Other and cannot escape. So how can you join us in conversations about the ideas in this book? If sales are modest you have the e-mails of the current authors, but if sales are better than this, then it may not be possible for us to answer you without ceasing to be able to work or to write! In such a case the answer is to join the network of those who appreciate this book and allow your messages to be passed on to the various authors according to the priority in each case.

Clearly it is high priority to take initiatives suggested in this book, especially in the UK, the Netherlands and in Germany where its three authors reside and we would love to help you make these succeed. We stand ready to do so. It is also important to explain in more detail what we propose and opportunities to speak, preferably paid, are welcome as are invitations to participate in what you plan to do. It is clearly lower priority to help you get published your dissertation on Criteria for Promotion in the Mexican Navy , or respond to suggestions of where we should shove our ideas. Were you to approach us via the networks to which we are connected, such messages might be given their requisite priority before being passed on to us. You can approach us via our publisher, Filament which is in Croydon, via the Big Innovation Centre, close to Westminster in London, or via The Institute for Leadership and Management in Tamworth, UK. Or via our consulting arm Trompenaars Hampden-Turner. You might in this way succeed in enlisting the support of persons at that address as well as ours and informing them of opportunities . The two co-authors are in FOM in Essen, Germany and in Amsterdam in the Netherlands and it might be better to contact them, depending on what you want done, where.

We are connected to a Blog, which for a limited period of time will be active. Were this to get too abusive we would cease however and in such circumstances you will have to approach us by indirection via the addresses below.

For Charles Hampden-Turner   chuckht@aol.com   He lives in Cambridge, UK
                              charleshampdenturnersenior@gmail.com
For Fons Trompenaars   fons@thtconsulting.com He lives in Amsterdam
For Linda O'Riordan   linda.oriordan@t-online.de She lives in Essen, Germany

APPROACH THE NETWORKS

Filament Publishing www.FilamentPublishing.com   16 Croydon Rd, Waddon, Croydon, Surrey CR0 4PA Tel. 44(0) 20 8688 2598

Big Innovation Centre   www.biginnovationcentre.com   20 Victoria Street, London SW1H 0NF Tel. 44(0) 20 3713 4036

The Institute for Leadership and Management www.InstituteLM.com   Pacific House, Relay Point, Tamworth B 77 5 PA Tel. 44 (0) 1543 266 866

Trompenaars Hampden-Turner Culture for Business www.thtconsulting.com Achillesstraat 89 1076 PX Amsterdam, the Netherlands Tel. 31 (0) 20301 6666

Linda O'Riordan   linda.oriordan@t-online.de FOM University of Applied Science Leimkugelstrasse 6 45141 ESSEN   Tel. 49 (0)201 81004-0

DEDICATIONS FROM THE AUTHORS

CHARLES HAMPDEN TURNER

Charles would like to dedicate this book to the Delancey Street Foundation in San Francisco and its two founders Mimi Silbert and John Maher – the latter sadly died while still young but the former has persevered and is my heroine. It taught me about the amazing unity that can grow out of diversity. What was I doing, thousands of miles from home, a graduate of Cambridge with a doctorate in business from Harvard, in a half-way house for ex-convicts and drug addicts? Yet those two years changed my life. I was exposed to people whose lives were sheer wretchedness, yet emerged with enough hope to last a life-time. If these people could turn their lives around, there was surely hope for us all. I had always been on the side of the under-dog but that particular kennel had begun to stink, the War on Poverty had atrophied and I was fighting despair. But when I fully engaged the members I realized that I could not have withstood the ordeals they had suffered and my admiration grew.

Quite suddenly ideas that I had been taught were poles apart, public and private, poor and rich, intellect and emotion, business and social relationships, Harvard and St Quentin, the culture of criminality and how to transform it, money and caring, critical detachment and passionate engagement, all came together in a new integrity that has sustained me ever since. There was one session of marathon group therapy that lasted three days and two sleepless nights. It began in sheer hilarity at the stupidity of life-styles, the thief crawling through the window who fell into the bath-water and was menaced by a bath-brush until the police arrived. It ended in tragedy for those who did not laugh at themselves in time. It culminated in a story of the death of a baby born to an addicted mother, after hours of agony. My two sons were born in the months before and the months after this narrative.

Never in my life had I realized just how lucky I was. It is not until you have descended into hell that you understand what heaven is. For value lies in the strongest contrasts as this book will show. It was Martin Luther King who said that until you discover something for which you would be prepared to die, you have not truly lived. His speech was played in the last minutes of the group therapy. We too, had a dream and it was coming true as we awoke.

LINDA O'RIORDAN

I dedicate this book to my Grandfather, Thomas Heaps, who understood that the greatest wisdom of all is first to love. In the hope that I can pass this spirit on to my son, Liam

FONS TROMPENAARS

For my wife, Cens

CAPITALISM IN CRISIS
VOLUME TWO

HOW TO MOVE TOWARDS A CIRCULAR ECONOMY

CHARLES HAMPDEN-TURNER,
LINDA O'RIORDAN,
FONS TROMPENAARS

Published by
Filament Publishing Ltd
16, Croydon Road, Beddington, Croydon, Surrey CR0 4PA
+44(0)20 8688 2598
www.filamentpublishing.com

Capitalism in Crisis - Charles Hampden-Turner - Volume Two
ISBN 978-1-912635-98-6
© 2019 Charles Hampden-Turner

Printed in the UK by 4Edge

TABLE OF CONTENTS

THE CRISIS OF WESTERN CAPITALISM: (VOLUME 2)
WHAT WE CAN DO ABOUT IT

INTRODUCTION TO VOLUME TWO

This volume responds to the challenge laid down in Volume One. There we argued that shareholders and the financial sector of the economy had become severed from stakeholders within companies who do the actual work and create the wealth we all enjoy. This has led to gross inequality with declining rewards for those working in the real economy on productive tasks. In turn, this has reduced salaries and wages and diverted funds from the most important contributors. We are less productive and innovative as a consequence. We have become obsessed with money as a mere means and are blind to the worthy ends to which it might be employed. Economic Man is bereft of purpose and meaning. These problems are all socially constructed by the way in which we think and we ended Volume One by criticising excesses wrought by these perceptions and advocated new mind-sets that promise to make us much more effective.

In this volume we will first address the subject of values in Part V. We will argue that values have scientific and verifiable meanings and it is possible to determine with great accuracy the kind of valuing that contributes to our integrity and the values that tear us apart. We criticise the contention of positivists that values are entirely subjective, have no testable meaning and are mere matters of taste, like the taste-buds on tongues. We believe this doctrine has betrayed generations of students and must come to an end. Once we have restored values to their proper place, we will see who in our society creates wealth and value and who does not, who threatens democracy and who supports it. All values are really differences and we need to reconcile these differences to remain civilized and in dialogue with one another.

In Part VI we turn to many different examples of how wealth has been created by outstanding companies. This has been done by creating additional wealth through the integration of values, not meaningfully connected before. Companies can and do marry low cost to high quality, although this is not easy. We see that companies reconcile change with continuity, competing with cooperating, wholes with their parts, standardization with uniqueness, rules with exceptions, errors with corrections, tasks with relationships, service with leadership, tasks with relationships among those tasks, formal with informal, productivity with people, action with reflection, authority with the empowerment of others, mass production with customization and so on. Reconciled values are scarce and scarcity enhances value. The values that have to be reconciled vary with the situation but in every case, it is the integrity of those values that wins the day.

In Part VII we advance the subject of creativity and innovation. We look at several approaches to that subject and note that while no two approaches are identical (that would not be creative!), all are made up out of paradoxes and dilemmas. All require highly contrasting values to be unified by the innovator and the company concerned. Innovation is the chief recourse for any developed economy since their higher wages makes competing with emerging economies difficult. But to innovate is to create at least a temporary monopoly until others catch up. We must innovate or die. Innovation is a way of life our cultures must learn. The capacity of human beings to make new connections among recently emerging developments is unlimited. We will never run out of ways to fascinate one another and improve the experience of living.

In creativity, old elements make new combinations and meanings, our minds focus but also wander, ponder and then pounce. We think divergently and brainstorm, only to converge on what has been thrown up. We reconceive questions to get new answers. We think vertically then suddenly make lateral connections between shafts. We immerse ourselves in money and then seek redemption through religious art. We play but with very serious intent. We doubt in order to become more certain, and we 'disorder' sets of ideas to find a new order among them. We create but then criticise and refine what we have wrought. We differentiate ourselves from others only to re-integrate. We invent but must then adapt and we let order emerge from seeming chaos. Once again, these values are contrasting to the point of paradox. The innovator must move between seemingly opposed values yet emerge with a new whole.

In Part VIII we apply the lessons of the first seven parts and come up with ideas on how to transform our economy for the better. We show how in several cases the environment has been saved while making handsome profits. Employees are more engaged in saving the environment than in making carpets, for example. We show that harnessing mankind to wind, tide and sunlight will soon produce energy the price of which will fall in perpetuity. We need not one bottom line but three, with People and Planet added to Prosperity. We can recycle and re-use worn out products and save on new resources; separating the ingredients is the clue. We can turn our cities into the green lungs of the earth with the Hanging Gardens of Babylon as our inspiration. Every flat roof needs a garden or renewable energy or both. The waste of one company can become the food of another by a process called industrial symbiosis.

We must create new alliances. One current alliance is between multinationals and NGOs. The latter are contracted to check up on and report the levels of social responsibility achieved by the former. We need claims to clean up the environment certified by those who care the most. Another alliance is between consumers who want to buy more than an object, and companies pledged to serve society. Can we purchase the character of that corporation, like Unilever's extensive campaigns to save infant children and improve public health? When choosing what to buy should we not remember this? The truth is we need for-profit companies, as only they have the power to scale up and globalize social concern. NGOs on their own are usually tiny and must beg.

Government can play an important part in these developments. China has clearly shown us the power of industrial strategies. Without this there is only defence and millions spent on better killing machines. Governments who act a Coach to their industries are far more influential than those who only Referee. To witness this, attend any football game and hear the insults hurled at referees. Governments should regulate us less and nudge us in right directions more. They are "choice architects" with the power to clearly label wrong decisions, such as smoking. They should advise us but not force us to lead healthier and fuller lives. The idea that government expenditures are a drag on the economy needs to be re-considered; every sharper spear makes the case for a stronger shield and vice versa. Apple's brilliant iPod used basic research funded by US government defence agencies - the internet was sponsored by the military! The military industrial complex has driven the US economy since preparations for World War I. It subsidizes high tech especially.

Governments in East Asia see products as connected. They subsidize those products which increase the value of other products, like microchips ('the rice of industry'), photovoltaic cells, electric car batteries, liquid crystal displays and so on. Potato chips and microchips are not of equal value. We need to calculate the true value of infrastructure projects. If traffic jams cost a country $20 billion, what is the value of halving this? If reduction in pollution halves admissions to hospitals for respiratory disease, how much is this worth?

We next look at how we must think differently. Not just closer relationships of greater mutuality but win-win relations of paradox leading to synergy. The secret of wealth creation is dynamic equilibrium between strongly contrasting values creatively combined. But thought is not enough - we have to act differently and create. We give several illustrations of successful action interspersed with suggestions of what might be done next. We finally stress the need to move from thinking to doing and feature the "Do Tank", the Big Innovation Centre and its several plans for action. Birgitte Andersen, its CEO, is working with several members of the British Parliament, both Commons and Lords, to suggest plans for action. We are in desperate need of improved socio-technical systems, that render technology socially benign.

PART V

THE SCIENTIFIC MEANING OF VALUE JUDGMENTS

A) FIGURE-GROUND RELATIONSHIPS

EVERY TEXT HAS A CONTEXT. EVERY PICTURE HAS A FRAME. EVERY FOREGROUND HAS A BACKGROUND.

One way we can express values is as figure-ground relationships, as illustrated opposite. Values have integrity so long as the two form a whole, a figure against a background, a frame around a picture, a text within a context, two sides of a Mobius strip. There can be no good without evil since these are contrasts, no you without me, no teach without learn. It takes both. Values can take it in turns to move to the fore and to the back. So that if I put You first, you may return the favour to Me. What I Learn now I can Teach later. If I wait by a traffic light the Red may feature against a background of Green and Yellow, before Green features before a background of Red and Yellow. The process is both circular and moves by turns from front to back. Values signal differences on a continuum. Note that contrasting values contain and constrain one another. Because of You, the assertion of Me will be kept within bounds. What I can Teach is limited and is constrained by what I have first Learned. It is important that values remain within the context of their contrasting values or they may cause mayhem. We will be distinguishing between values as end states and meta-values, which tell us how values relate to each other. We will examine a Frisbee as a useful metaphor or analogy. We will cite a series of reconciled values and the "flow experience".

We will show how and why absolute values get unhinged. We will consider the traffic light as a value system of universal adoption, look at the perils of adversarial relationships and examine theories of sequential levels of value synthesis and development.

TRUE VIRTUE LIES IN RECONCILED OPPOSITES:
VICE IS DISORDER BETWEEN

Draconian rules

Exceptions help improve rules

Rules battle
exceptions

Making
rules

Sheer anarchy

Discovering exceptions

IT IS LESS THE CONTENT OF VALUES THAT DEFINE VIRTUES, AS HOW THEY RELATE TO ONE ANOTHER.

A major theme of this book is that virtue lies not in values so much as between them. It is how a value relates to its contrast which decides whether or not it is pathological. Opposite we see that rules can learn from exceptions how to protect and help the development of more and more people, even those who are diverse. This is true of scientific rules making sense of data or of rules made by a legislature regulating the conduct of people. The elegantly dancing snakes top right, a symbol of healing among other things, show that rules allow and encourage people to be exceptional, which is what most of them want. The fiercely writhing snakes at bottom left, show what happens when rules rob people of self-expression so that they protest the rules. But those who police the rules then feel that law and order is threatened so that they try to crush those who take exception to the extant order. However, once you start fearing and impeding all those who point out exceptions, then rules get more and more oppressive and out of touch with the populace they are supposed to serve, while at the same time the populace may defy all rules, even wise ones, in their rage against the current order and anarchy threatens. When we start moralizing, conservatives generally insist on upholding rules, while liberals urge that exceptions and concessions be made to made to protesters who would not be so angry but for the war in Vietnam, Iraq etc. Both sides are right in the sense that no society without laws will work, nor will any society that fails to allow exceptions to be voiced and rules to be modified accordingly. No rules are universally true for ever more, and no protester is unambiguously on the side of life. We have to have a dialogue, and nations like Syria who cannot tolerate or discuss dissent, find themselves immiserated and resemble our mutually murderous serpents opposite. The end comes with neither a bang nor a whimper but with eternal verities upon a centrifuge, spinning savagely apart and justified by the "extremity" of the other.

SKILLS, CHALLENGES AND VALUES THAT FUSE AND TRANSCEND

JOY AND DISCOVERY OCCUR WHEN THE BORDERS BETWEEN VALUES COLLAPSE.

One of the greatest betrayals by teachers of students in our life-time is the refusal to give value judgments any descriptive and scientific meaning. They are regarded as nonsensical. Our contemporaries taught that you cannot get an "ought" from an "is", that value judgements are "exclamations of preference without any testable meaning" and should be left to clergymen and politicians. They were as intellectually significant as the taste-buds on our tongues. It is true of course that value judgements which ascribe all problems to human sinfulness do not get us very far towards solutions. Moralizing is too often an inhibitor of thought. But that we left students to confront the war in Vietnam without scholarly assistance casts shame upon us. Analytic philosophy chopped values into pieces and then pronounced them dead. True value lies in contrasts being fused and opposites transcended.

Mihaly Csikszentmihalyi researched life-long into human happiness. He found that this occurred when values suddenly flowed into one another. Take a work-team that has to solve a problem. This constitutes a challenge, see the vertical dimension. To this problem the team brings a degree of skill, lateral dimension. Much of this is inside the members and needs to be elicited *from* each member *by* fellow members. The fear is that the Challenge will be greater than the Skill, leading to Anxiety (top left). Alternatively, the Skill may be much greater than the Challenge, leading to Boredom (bottom right) But true value and great happiness results when the two flow together in a "whoosh" of joy, literally a "solution" as their permeable borders collapse in a flow experience. The challenge has evoked the skills, and the skills the challenges, as each value transcends its contrasting value in an intellectual-emotional surge of satisfaction. But it is fleeting and vanishes as mysteriously as it came upon us, leaving us still bemused.

❧

Values and Meta-values: Liberty and Fraternity weighed Equally

SOME VALUES LIKE EQUALITY, JUSTICE, RECONCILIATION, EMPATHY AND FAIRNESS, REFER TO THE PROCESSES BY WHICH OTHER VALUES FUSE.

We owe to Charles Handy the insight that Liberty, Equality and Fraternity are not the contradictory muddle of values that is often claimed. How can Liberty co-exist with Equality when people are so very unequal in their attainments? Those advocating equality are accused of wishing to reduce us all to an indistinguishable mass. Those advocating liberty are accused of defending the right to subordinate and oppress other people and so diminishing both fraternity and equality. Many conclude that these values have been simply thrown at us with no chance of cohesion or integrity. It helps to distinguish values from meta-values. Meta means "about", so that Equality as meta-value is about other values.

Opposite, we see Liberty and Fraternity weighed Equally. The case for Equality is not that we are all the same but that if we exercise the Liberty to be different, we need Fraternal relations in which these differences must be weighed equally to see which is best for particular situations. Even if someone is brilliant at mathematics compared to his sister, her skill at first-aid could save his life in an accident. We need to weigh these very different abilities equally to give each her/his due and to see that both are put to work in ways where each can excel and be fulfilled. So, far from equality demanding human homogeneity, it promotes human diversity and incomparability and promises an end to invidious distinctions. One of the gifts of fraternity is to allow each sister/brother as much liberty as possible.

❧

VALUES AS UPWARD SPIRALS AND SPINNING FRISBEES 1.

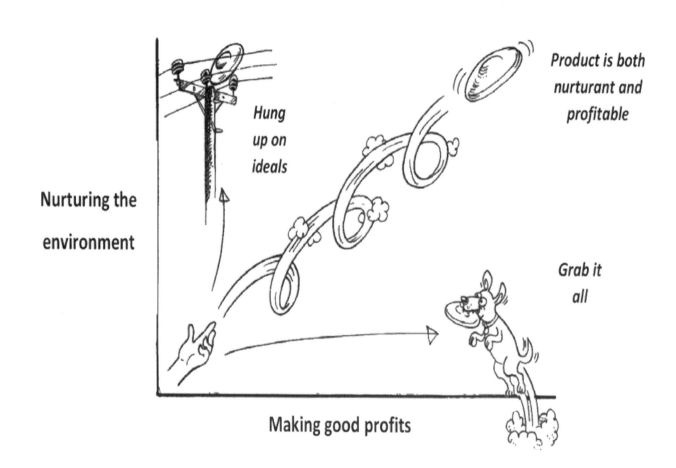

THERE ARE ALWAYS AT LEAST TWO WAYS OF COMING TO GRIEF IF YOU DO NOT SPIN THE FRISBEE AND FLY ARIGHT.

We owe to Theo Kroese the insight that values resemble Frisbees in several ways. The word comes from the Frisbee baking company in Connecticut before World War II. Pies supplied to schools came in tins, the lids of which were salvaged by children and thrown to one another. It took a few more years before these "lids" were deliberately manufactured. They need to be spun around in order to be directed in a straight line. The speed of this rotation determines the forward motion. They need to be on even keel. They have a near side and far side which change places as the disc spins. In the darkness these can have red and green lights, like a traffic light with hiccups. The sport is cooperative in the sense of being thrown within reach of your partner, yet competitive in matching your abilities to run and catch. There are always two ways of messing up, of veering off course and crashing.

Suppose you want to run a profitable business while being environmentally responsible. You can be very profitable yet litter the environment, see bottom right of picture, or be so environmentally conscious as to make no profit and bankrupt yourself, see top left. Or you can synthesize and synergize both values and make a profitable product that helps save the environment. To do so the values of profitability and environmentalism must be treated equally and balanced fairly against each other. Unless you make a profit, you will have no resources with which to sustain the environment. Unless you are environmentally responsible, today's profit is stolen from generations to come who must try to clean up a deteriorating planet and will curse your memory. Indeed, you have not made a genuine profit at all, but rather purloined a common heritage. Nor does the environment benefit in the least from you running out of money and yielding to a more ruthless rival. The helix is a most important trajectory, the stuff of life itself. Throwing a Frisbee joins mind to body, art form to science, energy to enjoyment, concentration to relaxation. Finally throwing, chasing, catching and returning a Frisbee is a partnership and a relationship on which the creation of wealth and value depend.

VALUES AS UPWARD SPIRALS AND SPINNING FRISBEES 2

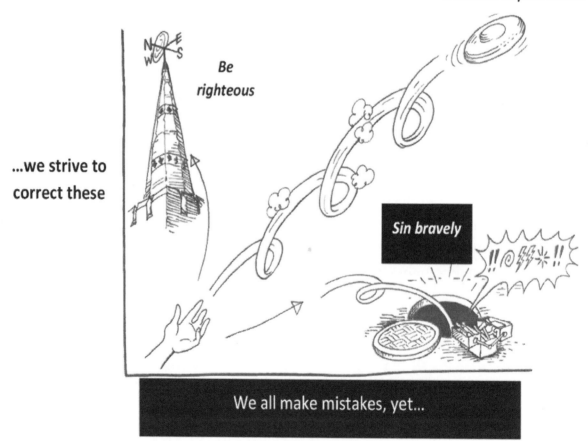

CORRECTION REQUIRES THAT WE FIRST ERR, AND HOW WE DEFINE ERRING, WILL DEPEND ON HOW HIGH WE ASPIRE AND HOW GOOD WE WANT TO BE.

Here again we use the Frisbee as a metaphor. Doing good and doing bad is a serious issue and many of us strive for righteousness. Yet we learn to love others by an extended series of corrected mistakes. What he or she likes or does not like, is a process of discovery with no science to guide us. Similarly what customers go for and do not go for is largely a mystery and they are not of one mind in any case. Eliciting the unique talents of your employees is also a voyage of discovery with unexpected twists and turns. We learn to solve problems, sustain customers, colleagues and members of our family by a process of successive approximations. We want to make them happy and watch their faces for clues. If mistakes were "bad" there would be no virtue in persistence and trying again and again. An Olympic athlete fails thousands of times before she at last makes it. Moreover the words "mistake" and "error" are hers to define. If she aims sufficiently high all her prior attempts will be "mistakes". Mistakes may even produce superior results to our deliberate efforts and intentions, in which case they may be adopted. We learn the most from "negative feedback" from what we did *not* expect and which took us by surprise. Without sinning bravely (bottom right) we can never make extraordinary discoveries. Righteousness (top left) makes us boring and conforming. Robert Louis Stevenson put it well. "If your morals make you dreary depend on it, they're wrong." What is required is constant improvement (top right) .

DIVERSITY OF VALUES AND THEIR RELATIVE MERIT?

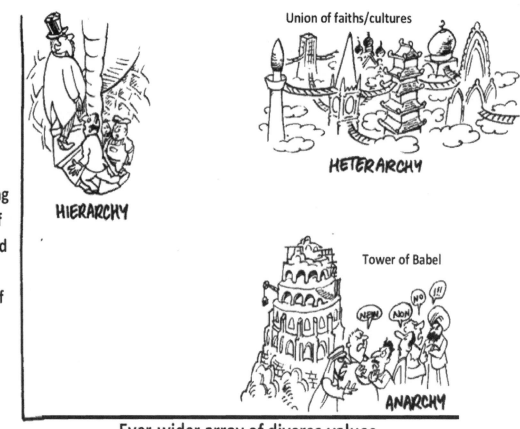

Ascending order of merit and league tables of worth

Union of faiths/cultures

HETERARCHY

HIERARCHY

Tower of Babel

ANARCHY

Ever-wider array of diverse values

WHERE PEOPLE ARE EXCELLENT IN INCOMPARABLE WAYS, ENVY AND RIVALRY REDUCE.

One problem with values is that we are for ever trying to prioritize them into some league table of relative human worth and getting them to compete with each other, so we will learn which is best. It does not seem to occur to us that this mania for hierarchical ordering reduces variety, diversity, alternative possibilities, uniqueness and the rich subtlety of distinctions. The world is many-splendored, not some grim race between standardized contestants who want the same scarce objectives. That said, too much emphasis on diversity and the idea that all values are just as good as each other, delivers us into anarchy (bottom right) and the Tower of Babel in which no one understands anyone else. Populist revolts against immigration are not without an underlying panic. People need to understand and be understood, and scores of unfamiliar faces make them unbearably anxious. They make racist remarks because they cannot understand themselves. Even so, the case for incomparably different values is strong. Who is best, a local football star or a woman who lost a leg in an accident and has trekked to the North Pole to raise money for fellow-amputees? These are so different that rank-ordering them is a waste of time and thought. We have Paralympics for this reason. We need para-values. We admire the woman because she has been disabled and is undaunted, while the football star is more exciting to watch. The problem with competition is that it favours existing public contests and ignores new, original developments. It is not until these new developments start to make money, that we approve of them. Is baseball better than scuba diving for undersea archaeology because it generates more money? To shrink activities to a cash nexus impoverishes our culture. According to Jay Ogilvy, we need neither hierarchy nor anarchy, but "heterarchy", a set of small pyramids, a union of cultures and faiths, a world of multiple perspectives that shares the truth among these. The case for equality is that people are different, not the same and we never know what difference might be useful in ever changing circumstances. Variety is the spice of life.

B) VALUES TAKEN TO ABSURD LENGTHS
UNIVERSALISM TAKEN TO TOO FAR.
LAWS SQUEEZE OUT RELATIONSHIPS.

WHY ARE THEY USING LAWYERS INSTEAD OF RATS IN ANIMAL EXPERIMENTS?

THERE ARE 22 MORE LAWYERS PER HEAD IN THE USA AS THERE ARE IN JAPAN. THEY KEEP EACH OTHER BUSY, AND MANY ARE IN CONGRESS.

Cultures take their favourite values too far. In the US it is law, the harness for self-interest, the policeman of the world, the judge of free markets and so spontaneous human relations suffer. There was a joke going around America a few years ago. You can rely on US culture to mock itself with exquisite wit. "Why are they using lawyers instead of rats for animal experiments?" There are three reasons. "1. There are more lawyers than rats. 2. The research assistants feel less sorry for the lawyers. 3. There are some things rats won't do!" The differences in the resort to the law by different national populations is very large. There are twenty-two times more lawyers per head of population in the USA than in Japan. The "rule of law" in much of Southeast Asia is said to be weak but if this means settling disputes among ourselves without the courts, it could be a major competitive advantage. One major reason that groups of foreign entrepreneurs avoid Western courts is they cannot afford to lose half their friends by taking sides in a bitter dispute. They appoint a respected member of their community to find a win-win solution.

Lehman Brothers sued a consortium of Chinese banks and won $300 million. Clearly their lawyers had outsmarted the Chinese in drafting the contract. There was only one snag. No one in the country would do business with Lehman thereafter and it had to withdraw. When the West visits China to do business it brings its lawyers, ready for the fray. These are met by party organizers planning convivial get-togethers and promises of friendship and mutuality. The latter system is much more flexible and adaptable to changing business circumstances. Where there is friendship the chances of both gaining are much better. It is your customer that makes you rich! Both of you need to succeed. The idea that one of you has to be "wrong" or has committed a tort for which she must pay, leads to protracted legal disputes and to those with the deepest pockets eventually winning a dispute. In the meantime, lavish payments to lawyers on both sides destroy wealth. The American sitcom *The Good Fight* features a serial killer who targets lawyers exclusively. The quickest way to repay your student loan is to go to Law School. Much of Congress consists of trial lawyers and their adversarial tactics polarize the whole country.

CONTRACTS TAKEN TOO FAR VS. RELATIONSHIPS OF MUTUALITY

THE CHINESE CONTRACT

THE THIRD ANGLE

TOMORROW'S COMPANY

The letter of the law to be imposed if necessary, compete legally

"SIGN HERE SO WE CAN FORCE COMPLIANCE!"

FIGHT YOUR CORNER!

"KEEP YOUR PROMISE IF IT'S CONVENIENT"

Friendly and flexible mutuality, both gain

IF YOU BOTH SEEK TO WIN, RELATIONSHIPS ARE BETTER THAN LAWS.

Charles Handy was negotiating an agreement on behalf of Royal Dutch Shell with a Chinese-Malaysian contractor. They got on very well indeed until Charles asked him to sign the document. Why was a signature needed, the contractor wanted to know? Had they not got on very well? Was the agreement not one by which both could gain. Why would friends force one another to comply if this proved inconvenient to either? Charles had a huge company behind him which could use the force of the law against a mere contractor but why would it want to do this? If the contract turned out to be a loser for either party should they not withdraw from it voluntarily? Did Charles want to force any losses on him? Up until this point, the contractor had trusted Charles to help both of them. Was it not better to keep the mutual understanding flexible so it could be modified at the request of either? The written contract was a memorandum of what they had agreed, but if circumstances changed should they not modify their agreement? Was not the point of a signature, to give most of the power to Shell?

We might consider the contractor naïve. of course, big publicly-owned companies require contracts. But did the contractor perhaps have a point? After all, Chinese-Malaysians are much wealthier on average than other Malays. As a minority they tend to avoid courts and litigating since the courts are likely to be biased against them. They resolve conflicts with fellow Chinese by informal agreement since they cannot afford rancour within their minority community. They could lose the friends on whom they must rely, so relations should be win-win if at all possible. The truth is that friendly relationships can be creatively adjusted while written contracts can be straight-jackets where circumstances have overtaken them. Why bind yourself by what you believed months earlier but is no longer so? Friendly, adjustable agreements are better. Charles sees *A Third Angle* where the contract brings clarity to cooperation, not coercion.

INDIVIDUALISM TAKEN TOO FAR: THE SOCIAL PURPOSE IS LOST

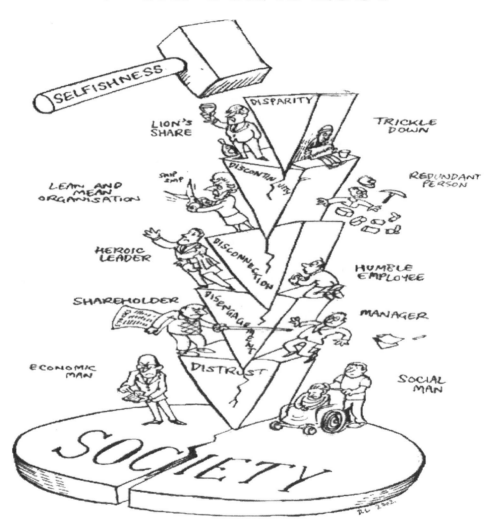

HAS ECONOMIC MAN GAINED ASCENDANCY OVER SOCIAL MAN?

The schema opposite are not our conception but that of Henry Mintzberg, who regards American and British societies as extolling individualism to the point of selfishness. It is true that Britain, the US, Canada and Australia are all much higher in preferring the individual over the group. Our research has established this. It is also true that individualistic countries pioneered the industrial revolution, but in this post-capitalist era, cultures that extol the community, like China and India, Singapore, Hong Kong, Taiwan and the Pacific Rim are growing much faster and have been doing this for a generation or more. Mintzberg sees an excess of individualism as sowing disparity between the rich and the poor and as purveying the myth that money trickles down, see top of illustration. A policy of austerity and cuts mean that people are redundant to skilled occupations and must join the hamburger flippers and the gig economy. We overpay the leaders of our distinctly mediocre organizations and the power of labour has been slipping for years. The shareholder is demanding more money from the manager or he will lose his/her company, while Economic Man has gained ascendancy over Social Man. Worst of all, our society is splitting and polarizing along this fissure, so that we have Trump in the USA and Corbyn in the UK. We will be encountering considerable evidence that wealth is created by close relationships among stakeholders and is largely the work of cohesive cultures. Especially successful have been Asian cultures with strong Western influences like Hong Kong and Singapore. The British provided many of the rules and the natives grew the economies through family-based Confucianism.

Atomism/analysis taken too far: whole meanings lost

Analysis is to whole meanings, what rubber and plastic objects in a sex shop are to grand passion.

We have seen in earlier pages that the secret of creating wealth and values is to see things whole. An elephant is not a collection of different images but a living whole. The cylinder is a fusion of two shadows, a rectangle and an ellipse. We need a division of labour but also its integrity. Once sexual intercourse gets separated from making love it turns to lust and often anger at the person being assailed. W.H. Auden wrote of his visit to the American southwest...

Come to our well-run desert/ where anguish arrives by cable
And the deadly sins may be bought in tins/With instructions on the label.

One problem with analysis and Newtonian atomism is the loss of whole meanings. We turn values into commodities, packaged, owned and accumulated - what Karl Marx called 'commodity fetishism'. A glance at the objects in a sex shop can be rather depressing. What is supposed to be passionate, committed and integral, has been rendered in objects of rubber, leather, metal and plastic. That the values we care most about can be represented by an arsenal of gadgets is a doubtful proposition. No wonder women complain of being sex objects! We obsess on their private parts to avoid the whole person. We once related to our bankers and trusted them to advise us. Today they sell us "financial products", sliced, diced and labelled with very doubtful probity. The person selling us a mortgage sells it on to strangers and does not want to relate to us. Big Data reduces us to bits and pieces of commodity to be mined like lumps of coal or iron ore. We are reduced to what we are likely to buy and our routine, unreflective behaviours are on sale to other advertisers. Vice is created by fragmentation and shattered pieces. Virtue lies in meaning, knowledge, wholes and connections.

c) VALUES AS WAVES WITH FREQUENCY AND AMPLITUDE

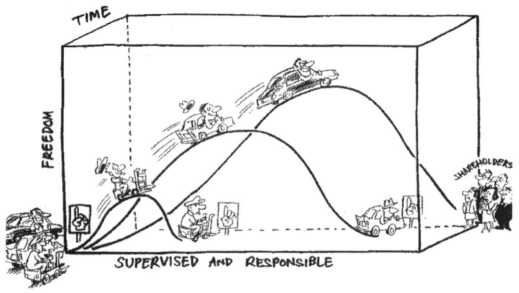

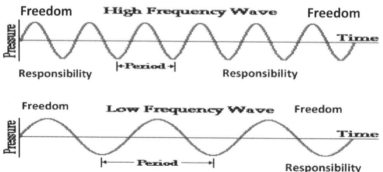

VALUES RISE AND FALL LIKE THE "OCEAN OF TRUTH" WHICH SIR ISAAC NEWTON WATCHED ROLLING BEFORE HIM.

We have seen that values figure in the foreground, then retreat to the background by turns. This is similar to wave-form with amplitude (height and depth) and frequency (how quickly crests and troughs follow one another). These are like the roll of the oceans. In the top picture we see Freedom on the vertical dimension and Responsibility to the person supervising you on the lateral dimension. For an hourly worker on a fork-lift truck, supervision is frequent, perhaps every twenty minutes. This leaves him some freedom and discretion but not much. He must be watched lest he make a mistake. The middle manager in the small car is held responsible every two months by having his work checked, but within these time intervals he is free. The CEO reports to shareholders when his contract expires in say – three years. Each of these people have mounting degrees of freedom and more significant responsibilities for longer periods of time, all the weightier for being delayed. This applies to all values. They rise and fall like ocean waves, 'I doubt now so as to verify later on. I risk money now to secure more in the bank later, as risk-taking builds security. I learn in order to teach and question to find answers. Because I have long loved my country and its people I must, like Socrates and Sir Thomas More, now dissent against its mistaken rules.' A recently promoted employee is given more freedom but must then give account for how she has used it.

THE TRAFFIC LIGHT AS A BENIGN FORM OF ARTIFICAL INTELLIGENCE

A paragon of good order

The stop light

(also a loop)

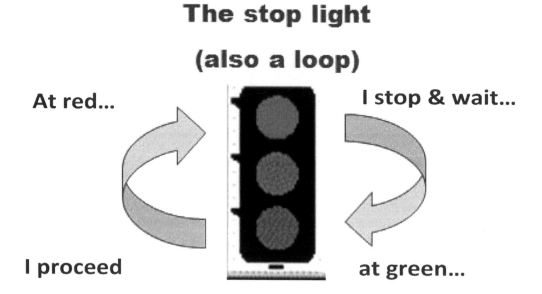

At red...

I stop & wait...

I proceed

at green...

IT IS THE MOVEMENT OF COLOURED LIGHTS BETWEEN STOP AND GO WHICH BRINGS ORDER TO TRAFFIC FLOWS. EITHER LIGHT ON ITS OWN COULD WELL PROVE LETHAL. GREEN MEANS OTHERS HAVE STOPPED FOR YOU. RED MEANS IT IS THEIR TURN TO PROCEED.

The traffic or stop light is one of culture's most brilliant inventions and illustrates how contrasting values form a loop. It also illustrates how cultures borrow from nature. We have borrowed from the colour spectrum that exists in nature and chosen two colours far apart and most contrasting to stand for a crucial difference - stop (red) and go (green). To the best of our knowledge it is used in every nation that has automobile traffic. What makes traffic controllable is the difference and the movement between red and green, not the colours per se. Values are dynamic. They move up and down or side to side over time. Were the traffic light to stick on red or green it would not simply be useless, but positively lethal and would actually help to cause accidents. Those stuck behind red would lose patience and attempt to cross right into the path of those released by green! This is an interesting analogy with absolute, fundamentalist, unchanging values. The signal can also adapt to traffic flows. Where a minor road crosses a major, the minor gets a 15-second green and the major road a 90-second green or thereabouts. Good values must be fair to everyone. There is only one respect in which this illustration of values is unlike others in this book. It is a machine and therefore dead. The red never gets any redder and the green never grows any greener. This does not apply to the living values in this book. The more profit you make for yourself, the more you are able to help others prosper. The better and more humbly you serve your cause, the more will that cause raise you up to a proud first place among your fellows. If you exercise your freedom well you will have discharged your responsibility. If you help Me I will help You in turn, and in time. We must not fear Artificial Intelligence, we must join together creatively to make it better and more humane

D) Values are reconciled in synergy or split apart

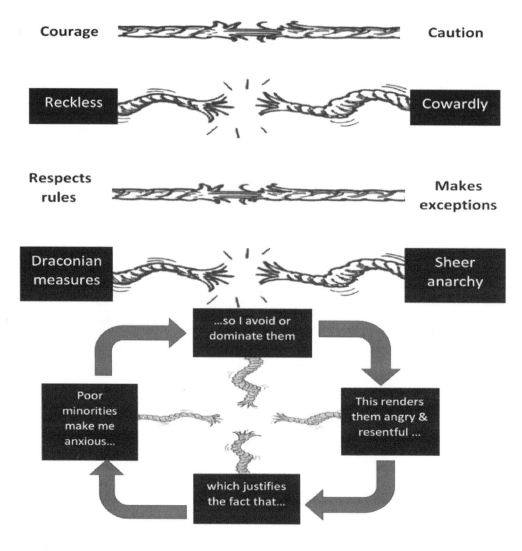

Courage — Caution

Reckless — Cowardly

Respects rules — Makes exceptions

Draconian measures — Sheer anarchy

...so I avoid or dominate them

This renders them angry & resentful ...

which justifies the fact that...

Poor minorities make me anxious...

"Only connect..." E.M.Forster

The difference between virtue and vice is whether contrasting values retain their integrity or come apart. Courage requires a measure of caution if you are not to get yourself killed. One reason for being courageous is to enjoy a more cautious life thereafter! Similarly, one must respect rules even when taking exception to these. Laws, whether scientific or judicial, are improved by noting exceptions to them and by subsequent reform. However, when respect for laws loses touch with exceptions, you get anarchy and draconian measures used to crush that anarchy. Just as courage becomes recklessness when severed, caution becomes cowardice. Shooting a helpless person is both reckless *and* cowardly. The lower image is of a vicious circle in which racial and class anxiety leads to a self-fulfilling prophecy as victims of domination become so resentful that this conduct is reinforced and many more minorities are jailed. The idea that value judgments are purely subjective is nonsense. They are structurally very different. As E.M.Forster said, "Only connect..." Every text must have a context, every picture a frame. The reason for caution is to conserve your courage and keep your powder dry. The rest of this section gives several illustrative examples of integral values and split values.

THE INTEGRATED VALUES OF DEMOCRACY

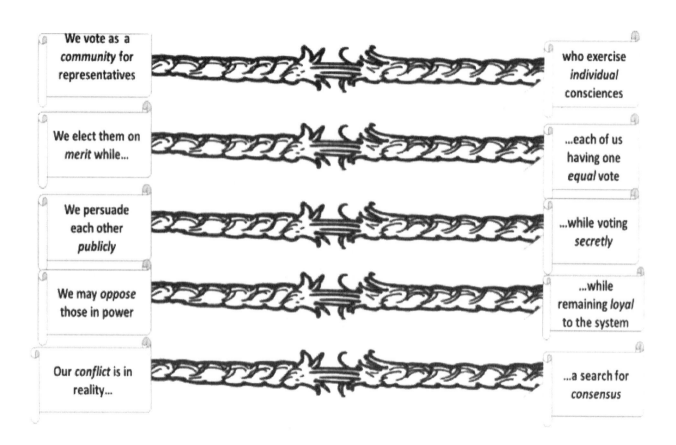

We vote as a *community* for representatives	who exercise *individual* consciences
We elect them on *merit* while...	...each of us having one *equal* vote
We persuade each other *publicly*	...while voting *secretly*
We may *oppose* those in power	...while remaining *loyal* to the system
Our *conflict* is in reality...	...a search for *consensus*

"YOUR REPRESENTATIVE IN PARLIAMENT OWES YOU NOT HIS INDUSTRY ONLY, BUT HIS JUDGEMENT AND HE BETRAYS YOU INSTEAD OF SERVING YOU IF HE SACRIFICES IT TO YOUR OPINION." EDMUND BURKE.

We have never succeeded in codifying the values of democracy. These are not seemingly rational and even seem to fly in the face of reason. We talk vaguely of checks and balances, of the separation of powers, of independent judiciaries, of equality before the law, of justice being blind, of indicted people being innocent, of prosecuting and defending but it is all strangely ad hoc. In Great Britain, the Mother of Parliaments, the values have never even been written down and seem to consist of tacit assumptions underlying ongoing conversations. But if we accept the paradoxical logic at the heart of this book it makes perfect sense and we must rally to its defence lest we lose it.

We vote as communities; not for a delegate but a representative who votes with her/his individual conscience. The community does not have to elect him/her a second time but they have had time to discover what that conscience has wrought, for good or for ill. The representative is elected on merit against an opponent, yet all voters have one ballot and an equal chance to define merit. Elections take place publicly as we try to persuade each other, yet we vote secretly lest those trying to bribe us or coerce us discover their success. There is a party or parties opposing the government and much of what it does, yet those parties are loyal to the nation's constitution and to parliamentary procedure. It is clearly a conflict, as was the decision to give women the vote, or to not prosecute homosexuals, yet such measures often lead to a new consensus of which democracy itself is an example. But look at the frayed nature of the ropes in their tension. Can we somehow disagree with everything another says yet fight to the death for his right to say it? This is no easy task and the bile and the rancour to which our politics has recently descended is a threat to us all. If your political opponent is really a crook and a foul conspirator, then it's all over anyway. Democracy relies on our having sincere beliefs and good intentions. Courts condemn crooks.

Soft values can provoke hard values: tragedy may result

The eternal verities go out on a centrifuge and destroy each other.

It was Gregory Bateson who explained schismogenesis, as "the growing split in the structure of ideas and values." He contrasted two kinds, the symmetrical, "anything you can do I can do better", especially Annie with her gun and the epidemic of school shootings, and the complementary kind, where hard values are excited to violence by soft values. We witnessed complementary schismogenesis during the non-violent Civil Rights campaigns. Southern segregationists lost their cool in front of TV cameras and clubbed kneeling demonstrators. Gandhi had pioneered this tactic in his great Salt March before the world's media. The more peaceful demonstrators gain with their open defiance of force and their flowers in gun-barrels, the more furious the soldiers or police become. The soldiers/police are being reproached as cruel, violent and barbaric and they know it. They did not even want to be here! They are keeping order, but readily descend into disorder themselves, as in the Chicago "police riot". It is often the demonstrators' intention that their opponents disgrace themselves, so neither side is innocent.

On the right, we have the famous scene from *A Streetcar Named Desire*, where Stanley Kowalski rapes Blanche DuBois. This is the culmination of her soft values provoking his hard values. The more precious, lady-like, class-conscious, vulnerable and reproachful she becomes, the more crude, brutish, proletarian, wounding and predatory he becomes. He will give her something to reproach! He splits externally and she splits internally, becoming schizophrenic, (the word means split-soul). This explains why too much of any one value polarity creates just its opposite. Peace marchers can evoke violence. America's universal lawfulness provoke mass suicidal attacks of no conceivable justification for such indiscriminate slaughter. When opposite values go out on a centrifuge, civilization crumbles.

RECONCILING SELF AND OTHER, EGOISM AND ALTRUISM

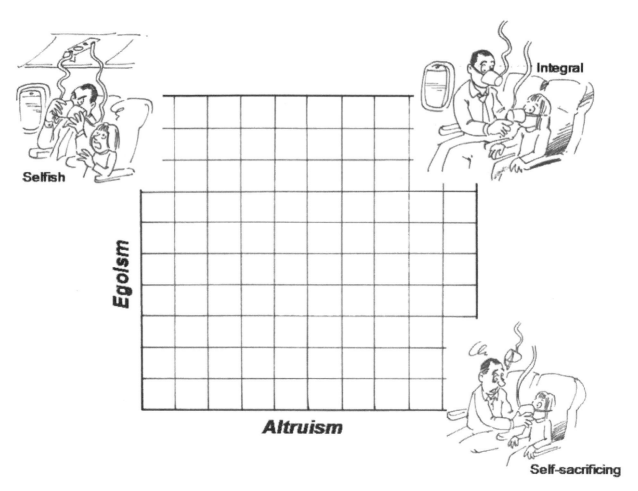

Selfish

Integral

Egoism

Altruism

Self-sacrificing

FIT THE MASK TO YOUR OWN FACE FIRST AND THEN...

Here is an illustration of how egoism and altruism work together. Many of us are familiar with the warning by airline companies that should the cabin suffer decompression, oxygen masks will fall from the ceiling. We are urged to fasten our own masks first and then attend to a child travelling with us. In short, first make sure you can breathe yourself and then assist others needing help. The point, of course, is to save both of you. (see the top right picture). It is not that your life is more important than anyone else's – most parents would disagree –it is that a fully functioning adult must take charge of the situation and if s/he cannot, both may perish. Not being able to breathe may disable you from assisting your child. Self-sacrifice (bottom right) could deprive the child of her father and threaten her life too, besides making the plane almost impossible to evacuate.   Altruism has broken apart from Egoism to produce Self-sacrifice. Egoism broken apart from Altruism to produce a Selfishness that could kill the child (top left). The two values are in a state of synergy or integrity at top right.

The swift sequence of actions is pragmatic. We can best take care of others when we have ensured we are fully equipped. When someone does you a favour you do not want to hear what that person had to sacrifice to do it, hence all the jokes about Jewish mothers! We too often assume that someone who has been killed defending the country has laid down his life for his friends, through "greater love," (John 15:13). Just ten minutes in a barrack room should cure us of such hyperbole! Aristotle was closer to the mark when he defined good luck as the arrow striking the man next to you. Brave people risk their lives and misfortune takes those lives away. If they want to die, they may be fanatics and too cowardly to face the world as it is.

COURAGE & CAUTION RECONCILED

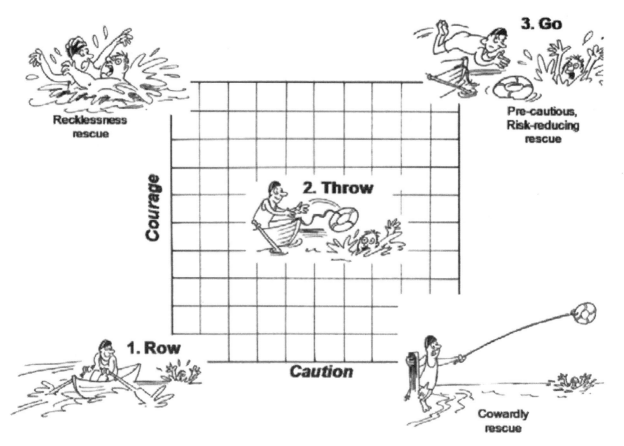

"ROW, THROW AND GO" IS THE STANDARD LIFE-SAVING DRILL IN THE US. HEROICS ARE NOT ENCOURAGED!

Socrates famously asked "What is courage?" and showed just how hard it was to define. He passed the problem down to us and we will do our best. The illustration opposite shows the dilemma faced by any life-guard on a beach. The record of coming to the aid of a drowning person is pretty dismal. Almost one third of the untrained perish in the attempt, so that sadly, two people, not one, drown. A near-drowning person will cling to you and drag you under the water with him. His desperate strength is ferocious. Going to his rescue unprepared is not courageous but reckless (top left), the name for courage which has lost touch with any caution. Similarly, if the life guard merely throws a belt from the safety of the shore this is not cautious but cowardly (bottom right). His caution has lost touch with his courage. American life-saving drill has an axiom; first Row your boat towards the person, then Throw the life-belt towards that person, and only if both these tactics are unavailing do you Go into the water yourself. This should be a last resort.

In short, Courage and Caution are finely joined and integrated and you may need both to carry out a successful rescue. One value without the other could prove lethal. The desire to be a hero must be resisted. Most life-saving is prosaic and ensures that your would-be rescuer survives. He or she are trained to break a death-grip on their bodies and bring the victim safely to shore. Once again, we see that vice and virtue are describable and are NOT "exclamations of preference" like the meaningless taste buds on our tongues. It is high time these descriptions were taught.

❧

Obedience and Harmony: Disobedience and Disruption

"Move fast and break things..."
Facebook's watchword

The Apple from the Garden of Eden with a bite out of it is of course the logo of that famous company. It stands for the fusion of obedience (to the natural world) and disobedience (to received opinion) without which knowledge cannot advance. In today's business to have disruption via innovative technology is almost a badge of pride. Facebook's motto used to be "move fast and break things". It stands accused of helping to break the democratic process by disseminating information on the existing opinions of voters so that they are manipulated and pandered to, rather than engaged and persuaded, turning leaders into pimps for private perversities. In truth there are no technical systems without lasting social impacts. Whenever we disrupt and disobey, we must do our best to restore a new and better harmony around that technology. Uber has a duty to the professional drivers it is displacing. They could easily be turned into guides for visitors and tourists and paid extra. Technology platforms have an obligation to protect children from paedophiles and to stop Internet trolls threatening assertive women with rape and murder. We are all destined to disobey but this does not alter the requirement that we help heal the social systems we have accidentally or deliberately gouged. Nature is a natural branching out, hence the symbol of the tree. Science is knowledge about nature, branching out from basic discoveries to thousands of commercial applications and technology off-shoots. Surely we have the wit to choose those innovations that will heal and help our social system and bring out the best not the worst in us? Anyone who explores nature knows of its unity, its elegance, its aesthetics and its wondrous order. Is it beyond our powers to combine our two sets of rules?

STEADFAST LOYALTY AND PRINCIPLED DISSENT

Loyalty to flag and country

Saluting the flag

Washing the flag

Burning the flag

Dissent against the cruelty of war

"PROTESTORS AGAINST THE WAR IN VIETNAM SHOULD NOT BURN THE AMERICAN FLAG; THEY SHOULD WASH IT." NORMAN THOMAS

At its best, protest and dissent is a lover's quarrel with your own country for acts you deem unworthy of it. You are angry because you love your country and believe it could and should behave much better. The image opposite comes from the words of Norman Thomas, the American socialist politician. He told protesters against the Vietnam War that if they did not want to salute the flag (top left) and pledge loyalty to the nation, then they should not burn the flag in public demonstrations (bottom right) as they had been doing, but should wash the flag in an attempt to retrieve the nation's honour and reputation. He was never elected to office – perhaps he was before his time. But surely he was correct. We voice dissent because we love and care for the nation that includes family, neighbours and our friends within it. If our nation was beyond redemption we would have to give up. A dissenter who does not care is a potential traitor, just as a loyalist who does not care may commit mass murder. In the face of white phosphorus and Agent Orange it is hard to keep both contrasting values in mind, but it is the measure of our humanity that we must do so. If we stop believing in words there are only weapons left and our opponents may handle these with greater ruthlessness than we do, as in 9/11.

SOLITARY APPEALS TO SOLIDARITY: THE ME-TOO MOVEMENT

THOSE WHO TAKE A LONE STAND AGAINST INJUSTICE HAVE ALL THOSE WHO EVER LOVED THEM, GHOST-LIKE AT THEIR SIDE. "I REBEL, THEREFORE WE EXIST." ALBERT CAMUS

Albert Camus wrote the story of the dying artist who had painted his last magnificent canvas. He had signed it in the right corner "Solitarism". Except that some admirers of his work claimed it was "Solidarism". (Both words are in French). There ensued an argument about what the famous artist had really meant and what he wanted to say with his signature. Was the letter a "t" or a "d"? Had his paintbrush slipped? Camus was trying to get us to see that solitarism, brought about by a lonely act of conscience, leads to human solidarity. You stand for what you believe to be right, risking scorn, rejection and ridicule, but then you suddenly find yourself leading a movement of those who suffered the same fate but never dared to defy the power of those with more authority.

A recent example of this is the film stars and others in the industry assaulted by Harvey Weinstein, see picture on right. He had the power to make or break the career of the woman he groped. It was common knowledge that he did this and then paid hush-money but still no one would confront him. His response and that of his backers and lawyers could doom her career and any chances of a part in the movies he made. Yet once a stand was made by Tarana Burke, Alyssa Mulano and others, the Me Too movement was born and the ranks of accusers were simply too large to ignore. The scales tipped decisively against him. Incidentally, it also works the other way around. Those close to their own families, their mothers especially, are more likely to refuse to torture a victim when ordered to do so by a fake scientist, feigning research on "the effect of pain on learning," and who orders electric shocks be administered to a fake victim who writhes in pain and eventually pretends to pass out. Those refusing to do this had much higher social skills and more stable human relationships.

᷍

CRITICISING AND SUPPORTING EMPLOYEES

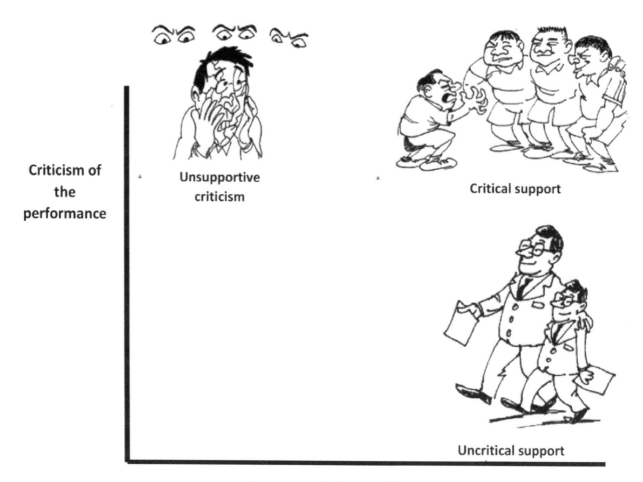

Criticism of the performance

Unsupportive criticism

Critical support

Uncritical support

Support of the performer

IF YOU TRULY SUPPORT YOUR SUBORDINATE YOU CAN NEVER BE CONTENT WITH HIS/HER PERFORMANCE.

Surely you either criticise the employee or you support him? You cannot have it both ways. Has he done a good job or not? Yet the answer is that you must do both. Let us first see what happens when you give unsupportive criticism as at top left. The figures are Asian because they are more likely to have shame cultures, wherein criticism is public and the individual "loses face", (see it crumbling beneath hostile stares). He is unlikely to benefit from this since you have made him feel incompetent and his subsequent performance may be even worse. He feels that you reject not just his work but him as a person. He will probably want to quit. An alternative is to give him uncritical support, bottom right. This may cheer him up but if his work has not been good than your support is unlikely to improve it and he is likely to become a clone of the person supporting him, see bottom right. Some women get uncritical support at work from male supervisors, who feel that being unfailingly nice will fend off any complaint. But this denies women the chance to improve since they are not told of any short-comings. The only answer is to integrate both values so that you support the performer but criticise his/her performance. You say in effect, "I respect you and your potential and I know you can do better than this." No one can improve if their morale is destroyed (top left). No one can improve if they are not told they can and should do better (bottom right). They must be given enough support so they keep trying and rally from any set-back. Once again we find that the clue to high performance is found in relationships among people and among their values. The person is supported but their work is constructively criticised.

COACHING FOR DIVERSITY AND INCLUSION

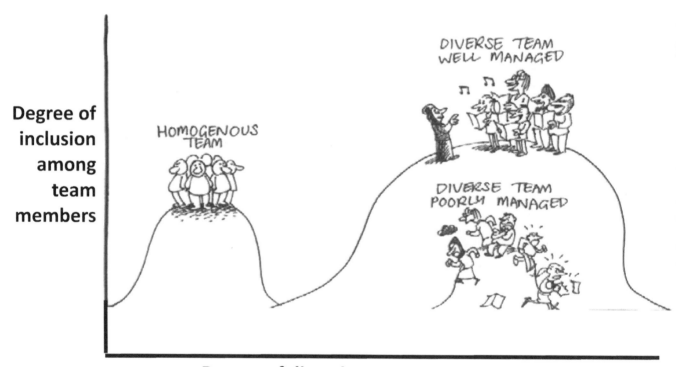

DIVERSITY BY ITSELF HAS LED TO LYNCHINGS AND PURGES. THOSE WHO ARE DIFFERENT MUST BE INCLUDED AND ENGAGED.

Diversity by itself is not a virtue. Indeed it can be positively dangerous. Where diverse people are not also included in the culture, they are likely to be marginalized, persecuted and even annihilated. The idea that diversity on its own is "good", needs critical re-examination. Research by Joseph DiStefano and Martha Maznevski shows that diversity in the membership of a team is a risk leading to both gains and losses. Diverse teams do much worse and much better than homogeneous teams, depending on the quality of management. In the picture we see that homogeneous teams (left) do passable if not spectacular work. They are unlikely to engage in serious conflict as their values are so similar and communication among them is unlikely to break down. However they are also less likely to be creative, since new ideas from unfamiliar people are necessary for this to occur. If, on the other hand, you have a very diverse team, then serious disagreement is more likely because of the distance between members, see bottom right. The team may even break up into angry factions and fail to come up with a viable solution. It takes social skills and high managerial competence to orchestrate a very diverse team so as to get full benefit from its rich variety of viewpoints. However, if we want spectacular results this is the only way.

Private enterprise is a risk-reward equation. You make profits because you have borne risks and getting diverse people to work with one another is yet another of these risks. We also need to be clear about different kinds of diversity. While it is self-evidently fair to include women and ethnic minorities, their colour or gender do not by themselves lead to creative excellence. Some minorities try to make up for their visible diversity by chronic comformity, as when women ape the macho conduct of men. We need a diversity of values and perspectives for excellence to arise. Different life experiences must be authentically expressed.

≪ട

E) WORLD VALUES ARE MIRROR IMAGES OF EACH OTHER 1)

A MIRROR SWITCHES A PAIR OF VALUES
AND ALTERS THE CULTURAL PRIORITY.

There are two definitions of globalism. One insists that we should all be the same and resemble the USA, which sets the rules and enforces these with defence expenditures amounting to the spending of the next five countries put together. The second definition is that we share the truth between us and must engage in dialogue and mutual understanding. Given the economic growth rates in East Asia, they clearly know something we have missed. It is time we started listening rather than simply proclaiming our own superiority and insisting every other nation measure up to our values. Fons Trompenaars and Charles Hampden-Turner have measured the values of managers in 76 nations. The largest differences are between the USA, UK, the white ex-Dominions and South East Asia plus India. These resemble two sets of rival values but they are in fact single value continua with contrasts at each end. There cannot be individuals without community. There cannot be rules without exceptions. These values help define each other. They are the two sides of one mirror through which we must step to engage each other. Trompenaars located the following differences.

Preferred by the Anglo-sphere	Preferred by East Asia and India
Universal rules	Particular exceptions
Individualism	Community
Analysis into specific parts	Relating into diffuse wholes

WORLD VALUES ARE MIRROR IMAGES OF ONE ANOTHER 2)

"WHY IS SATAN LEFT-HANDED (OR SINISTER)?" GREGORY BATESON

If you look at your own face in the mirror and you have a beauty spot or dimple on your right cheek, the mirror will move it to the left of your reflected image. It is the same with values. On the other side of the globe people have the same values as we do but with different relative emphases. While the UK, the USA and Northwest Europe, tend to put Universal rules (UN) before Particular exceptions (PA), China, South Korea, India and others reverse this and regard their people and their circumstances as exceptional. Rules made by Americans have limited appeal. While Americans tend to be Individualistic (IN), as a nation of immigrants often is, preselecting the most footloose and independent, rice-growing cultures are far more Community oriented (CO). If there are not enough of you to grow rice, you die. War and social disorder brings starvation to millions. SP stands for specific objects, data and items, typically produced by analysis, while DI stands for diffuse wholes, relations and connections typically created by synthesis and patterns.

Value systems require all of these in order to work effectively. The individual is vindicated when the community confirms her service. The community is vindicated when it raises an independent individual. You cannot analyse things to pieces without restoring the whole, and wholes can become totalitarian. Rules are improved by noting exceptions and do we not all wish to be exceptional rather than compliant? Despite the fact that human beings face the same sets of contrasting values, we get very suspicious when foreigners seek a balance different from our own. But America would not have survived and prospered without its individualism. This fitted the circumstances its people found. China would not have survived and prospered without its community orientation. Wars are too costly. Rice needs at least a village to sow and harvest. None of this means that Americans never cooperate; of course they do. Just as Chinese individuals succeed as entrepreneurs. We are talking of the relative weight placed on pairs of values and we need to understand that cultures have unique histories. Each culture tends to overplay its strong suit, with Americans individualistic to the point of alienation and the Chinese communal to the point of coercion. If we want to create wealth and grow, we must rather learn from each other.

f) Developing Values at Higher Levels of Integration

"I SUBMIT THAT THE INDIVIDUAL WHO BREAKS A LAW THAT CONSCIENCE TELLS HIM IS UNJUST, AND WHO WILLINGLY ACCEPTS THE PENALTY OF IMPRISONMENT IN ORDER TO AROUSE THE CONSCIENCE OF THE COMMUNITY OVER ITS INJUSTICE, IS IN REALITY EXPRESSING THE HIGHEST RESPECT FOR LAW." MARTIN LUTHER KING

Lawrence Kohlberg estimated the level of moral reasoning which a person has reached by presenting her/him with a dilemma. Your husband/wife is dying of a disease curable by an expensive drug which you cannot afford and for which the druggists demands full payment. The test is of moral reasoning – most people appropriate the drug. At level 1 you fear punishment, possibly from his/her relatives. At level 2 you insist that s/he is instrumentally useful to you and you will have your way. At level 3 you define yourself as "a good wife/husband" and act accordingly. At level 4 you cite Law and Order. You are required to protect your partner (or not rob the druggist). At level 5 you cite your voluntary personal commitment to him/her and argue that this directs you to rescue your beloved partner. At level 6 you exercise your personal conscience. You will appropriate and administer the drug, accepting any penalty imposed, not just for the sake of your partner but for all those too impoverished to pay the price of rescuing those they love. No decent society should let this happen. If you are jailed so be it. You must bear witness to an intolerable situation. Note that this act of conscience can lead to new interpersonal commitments among Civil Rights activists, (level 5), to a new Civil Rights Act (level 4), to new definitions of a "good partner" (level 3) and so on. Our laws protect acts of protest and associations whose members may freely assemble and commit to each other. Legislation may be guided by conscience, as in the abolition of the death penalty and the freedom of homosexuals to love each other. Note that every successive stage integrates the values of lower stages at a higher level of integrity. Also, every higher step is the reconciliation of the dilemmas among stages beneath it, so that Following your Conscience (6) is a reconcilation of Interpersonal Commitment (5) and Law and Order (4). Even where the law punishes that commitment you will respect it and explain your reasons.

❧

SUCCESSIVE STAGES OF INTER-CULTURAL SENSITIVITY

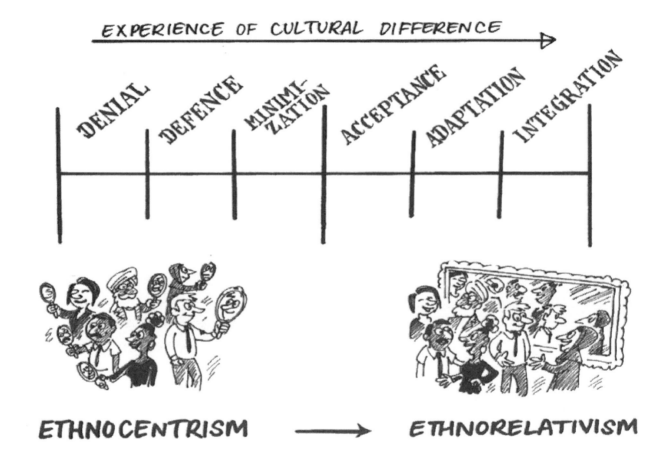

EXPERIENCE OF CULTURAL DIFFERENCE

DENIAL   DEFENCE   MINIMI-ZATION   ACCEPTANCE   ADAPTATION   INTEGRATION

ETHNOCENTRISM → ETHNORELATIVISM

"DO UNTO OTHERS AS THEY WOULD WISH TO BE DONE BY."
THE PLATINUM RULE

We have seen that engaging people of different cultures can lead to tension amounting to anxiety, but lesser tension can be experienced as excitement at new experiences, a motive behind much tourism. Milton Bennett's research has shown that people develop through stages in their capacity to engage and to learn from persons different from themselves. People begin as ethnocentric, as believing that their community, religion, ethnicity, skin colour and culture is right and normal by definition and all other people are deficient to the extent that they deviate from this. They see themselves as a reflection of what is right and proper. They grow in ethno-relativism, that people's values are relative to their situations and their social environments and that we can learn from this.

Bennett sees six stages. The first is Denial of any difference or any complaint about this. The victim of discrimination is often forced to pretend to happiness and act in guileless and child-like manner, as once did many blacks in the American South. "We wear the mask that grins and lies...". At stage 2, you get Defence. "Yes they are different from me but that has everything to do with inferiority and their degree of difference spells out just how inferior they are. To protect myself and white Southern womanhood I must dominate, even intimidate." The next stage. Minimization, also admits to differences but minimizes these; we are "all God's children", all citizens of this country, all really the same beneath superficial appearances. We should be colour blind. Note that the Golden Rule assumes we all want to be treated in the same way! At stage 4, Acceptance, we start to admit that people are legitimately different with a right to their own values. At stage 5 we are willing to Adapt ourselves to these values, especially when visiting, "when in Rome.." etc. Only at stage 6 are we willing to Integrate some of those values into our own systems and live these. Bennett proposes a Platinum (not Golden) Rule. "Do unto others as they would wish to be done by." We have to accept that people are legitimately different.

TROMPENAARS' FIRST TWO DIMENSIONS

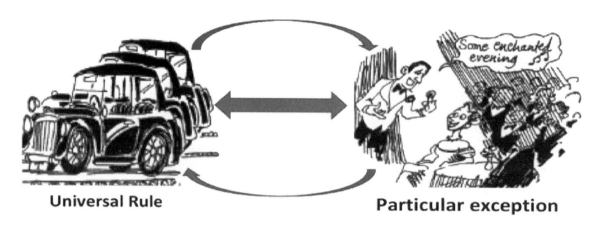

Universal Rule ⟷ **Particular exception**

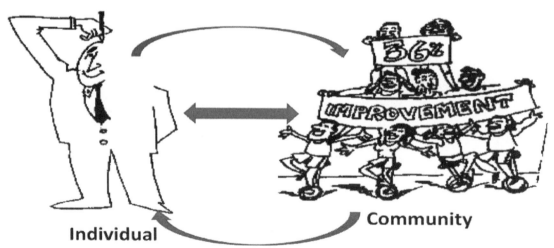

Individual ⟷ **Community**

THE EXCEPTION PROVES THE RULE.
"IT TAKES A VILLAGE TO GROW INDIVIDUALS."
HILLARY RODHAM CLINTON

Fons Trompenaars measures cultural values by presenting respondents with dilemmas. When your best friend speeds in his car with you as a passenger and injures a pedestrian, do you protect your particular friend or do you honour universal truth by testifying in court and on oath to his/her guilt? Protestant Western countries tend to uphold the rule. Confucian countries stick with friends and Catholics countries are in the middle. This also applies to products. Hens' eggs are standardized and rule bound. Fabergé eggs are particular with the value of being unique. We asked whether managers liked to work as individuals or as a group. The difference was largely as before. Protestants approach God singly. However, when it comes to effective cross-cultural competence, every rule needs to take note of exceptions and exceptional people set standards of attainment. You should urge your friend to tell the truth while supporting him/her. You should manage group members in such a way as to uphold the individuality and creativity of each member. Values dance in circles or side to side on continua. They harmonize. We become better individuals through groups. The group excels because it has given individuals encouragement. Our laws get better because we have examined exceptions and improved the rules so they cover more instances. Women tend to be more on the right side of the page, like Asians. Men tend to be on the left.

❧

A SECOND PAIR OF DIMENSIONS BY TROMPENAARS & BERLIN

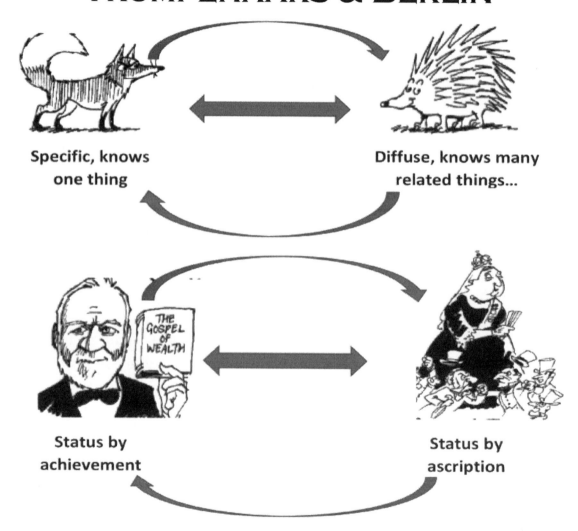

Specific, knows one thing

Diffuse, knows many related things...

Status by achievement

Status by ascription

"HE WHO WOULD DO GOOD MUST DO IT IN MINUTE PARTICULARS." WILLIAM BLAKE

Isiah Berlin is famous for his distinction between the Hedgehog and the Fox. The Fox is specific, objective, factual; he "knows one thing" and analyses situations into discrete units. The Hedgehog thinks diffusely and is concerned by the whole and the relationships which unite the many spines which converge upon his body. Western powers think like foxes and those do who not, like communists and Marxists, risk totalitarianism with its unverifiable theories. East Asian countries think more like hedgehogs and focus on relationships. Women managers are also more concerned with relationships than are men. Trompenaars asked his samples whether a corporation was a set of tasks, machines, and monetary rewards, or more like a web of relationships. Western male managers chose the specific tasks, East Asians chose the diffuse web. Once again it is possible to bridge this divide. Meaning tends to reside in larger wholes yet the details are very important and "he who would do good must do it in minute particulars," as William Blake pointed out.

Should we give status to those who achieve like Andrew Carnegie and his Gospel of Wealth, (lower left of illustration)? Or should status be ascribed to people so they stand above the political fray for the values that unite a nation? Once again the answer is both. If we did not ascribe status to those who clean up the environment, the Cigarette Millionaire would rule unopposed. There are feats worth achieving which monarchs often symbolize, and feats not worth achieving, Ascribed values are at the root of all cultures, shaping the people and what they stand for. In China the communist party ascribes value and the private sector achieves these. It works after a fashion.

TROMPENAARS LAST TWO DIMENSIONS

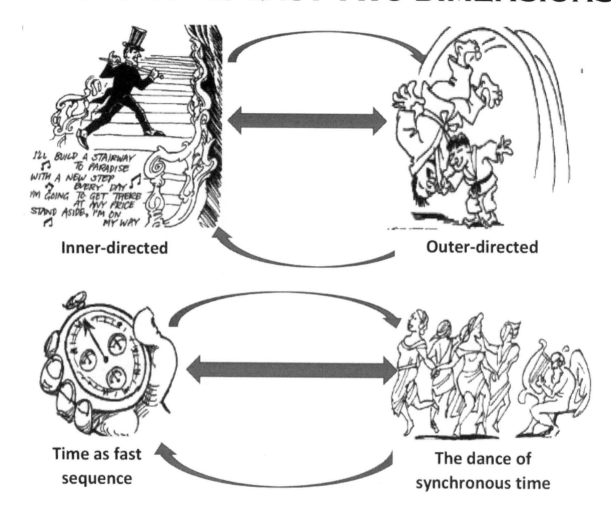

Inner-directed

Outer-directed

Time as fast sequence

The dance of synchronous time

"I AM THE LORD OF THE DANCE" SAID HE.

Cultures vary in the extent of their inner-directedness, steered from within by conscience and will-power, or their outer-directedness, steered by people, patterns and nature outside of us. Do you "Build a stairway to paradise" by dint of your own efforts? Or do you use judo and indirection to outwit you opponent, borrowing his momentum? America's romance with guns is an example of inner-direction. You pull a trigger and an instant later your opponent is dead and the most trigger-happy and prejudiced will shoot first. Guns make bigots of us. While inner-direction is often part of individualism, it need not be so. The French are community-oriented and very inner-directed; groups of French people moved by inner convictions have changed that nation. Needless to say, the two values oscillate back and forth. When a handful of people express revolt (inner-direction), they may be joined by thousands (outer-directed). The West tends to be a "talking culture" and the East a "listening culture", which could explain why they threaten to surpass us. They learn faster by listening. Britain and America invented mass manufacturing and time-as-a-sequence (lower left). The Japanese invented just-in-time processes, or time as a synchronized dance (lower right).. But these also fuse in Time-as-an-ever-faster-dance. While we dash down the race-course, much of East Asia creates two race-courses in parallel and then integrates their outputs. Modern factories can produce thousands of different products because one assembly line has met another "just in time". The dance incorporates the rapid sequences. Japan learned from us (outer-directed). We failed to learn from them being too busy issuing inner-directed instructions to everyone else. Manufacturing is a major source of earned economic growth We have neglected and outsourced this to our peril. Once again, women tend to be more synchronous than men and can famously multi-task.

PART VI

ILLUSTRATIONS OF WEALTH CREATION

Combining Opposed Values

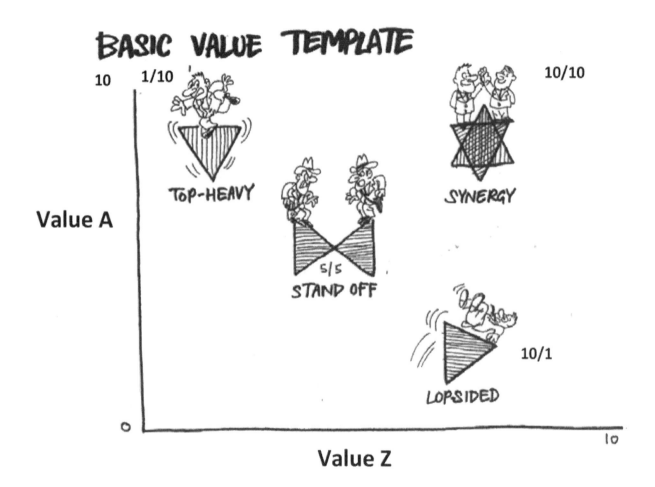

BASIC VALUE TEMPLATE

10   1/10   10/10

TOP-HEAVY

Value A   5/5

STAND OFF   SYNERGY

                                             10/1

                 LOPSIDED

o   10

Value Z

We shall be using the basic value template above to show how wealth is created by companies

This is the basic template we will be using for all illustrations of how wealth is created by companies in this section. They succeed to the extent that contrasting values, symbolized by A and Z, are aligned synergistically (from syn-ergo, "to work together"). Relationships between people and their values must be optimal. Too much of Value A destroys wealth by being top-heavy. Too much of Value Z destroys wealth by being lopsided. In the middle, values are compromised (Stand-off). In Synergy each value sustains and increases the other. It is not easy but it is possible. We start with the Formal System of an organization – what employees are required to do - and the Informal System - what workers do spontaneously to make their workplace more bearable, even pleasant. In the famous Hawthorne Experiment these unexpectedly fused with amazing results. We next turn to a deliberate exploitation of Hawthorne's results by the Managerial Grid, by teams which grow over time, by the application of Theory Y, by the application of fate-sharing and gain-sharing teams. We look at an application of Hawthorne ideas at Anheuser Busch. We then look at how fusing various contending values helps, i.e. low-cost standardized products with high quality premium products, change with continuity, competing with cooperating, rules with exceptions, abstract with concrete, action with reflection, time-as-a sequence with time-as-synchronization and parts with wholes and so on.

⤌

A) Teams and relationships: Hawthorne and the informal system

The Formal system. What the women employees were required to do.

The informal system: What changes emerged spontaneously

How the formal and the informal systems accidentally fused.

One of the oldest ideas in management science is that employees should do precisely what they are told and it only remains to see what the best of all instruction tools look like. Managers give direct orders, helped by a "science" of perfect prediction and control. That was how the Hawthorne Experiment at Western Electric in 1927 began. Immigrant women employees of Irish and Polish extraction, not long off the boat, were taken out of the factory and put in the Relay Assembly Test Room where they put together telephone relays around a table. The heights of table and seating were raised and lowered, as was the illumination, the rest periods, the quality of food and drink, the interval of rest periods and the amount of pay received. Their output was communicated to the women at the end of each day. The researchers soon became excited because those independent variables were working! Productivity kept climbing whatever new variable they tried. But then they took them all away and reverted to the status quo ante. Behold, productivity was still 39% up! So those variables were not working at all. Something else was happening. What was it?

In the first place, they were being carefully observed. But to the women, this meant respect, from the Latin respicere, "to look at". Their foreman was barred from the room because his tirades upset them. The researchers wanted them treated "normally" - as Harvard would treat research assistants! The small group of women came to like each other and since assembling relays is mindless they could all talk and befriend each other. The nice men who treated them so politely seemed very pleased whenever productivity rose, so why not give them what they were looking for? After all, several of the hypotheses they were testing would make life better and now the women were in control of output! Also, the researchers were very interested in why they were working better - the more they told them the more productivity rose. Assembling telephone relays is routine, but discovering how they might be better assembled is important research. And then there were the distinguished people who came to see them and peered in, a great accidental discovery! Even so the point was missed. Motherly women were hired to counsel workers and sat in sheds near the factory to listen to their complaints and so placate them. Managers had other priorities!

THE MANAGERIAL GRID: FUSING PEOPLE WITH TASKS, ARTS & SCIENCES

WHAT IS REQUIRED IS CONCERN WITH PEOPLE THAT RENDERS THEM MORE PRODUCTIVE, CREATIVE AND RESPONSIBLE.

The Managerial Grid is the work of Robert Blake and Jane S Mouton who left the University of Texas to found their consultancy. As with Hawthorne, it concentrates on teams, in this case managers, not workers, and has them assess one another on Concern with People, (horizontal axis) and Concern with Production (vertical axis}. The individual rates him/herself and is then rated by other team members. Any disparity causes some shock and a desire to improve their ratings. The orientation to people is associated with liberal arts. The orientation to production is associated with science, technology and engineering. If Concern with People is taken too far you get the culture of the Country Club (bottom right). This has lost touch with the tasks that must be performed effectively if the company is to prosper. If Concern for Production is taken too far you get the culture of the Sweat Shop (top left). It has lost touch with people and their humanity and is driving them relentlessly. You will get hostile reactions and fail to get the best out of people. What is required is a Concern with more Productive People, or a socio-technical system that organizes people around changing technology. The USA and the UK both oblige university students to specialize in arts or sciences. This tends to produce unbalanced people with biases towards things or people. You have to fuse *both* approaches to be successful. The Grid is the formal part of the exercise but the interaction of team members is the informal part and will throw up many spontaneous reactions of members to each other. The team develops over time as it fills up with information about mutual interactions and the strength/weakness of key relationships. Towards the end, much time is spent on discussing improvements back in the company from which members are drawn. These workshops were popular for many years but their reputation went before them, so people knew in advance what values were required and therefore tended to feign these.

Teams tend to develop over time

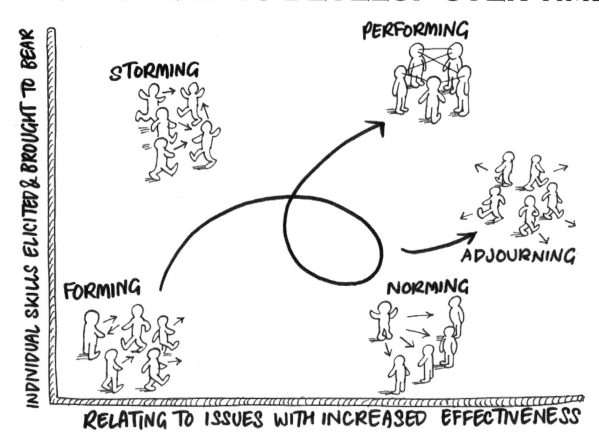

A TEAM OF STRANGERS, AS THEY LEARN ABOUT EACH OTHER, GROW RAPIDLY MORE EFFECTIVE AND COMBINE DIVERSITY WITH INCLUSION. THEY ALSO BRING THE INTIMACY FORGED AMONG THEM TO THE SOLUTION OF COMPLEX CONFLICTS AND PROBLEMS.

What happened in the Hawthorne experiment was that the team of women developed over time. Team development is a phenomenon apart from the development of individuals in that team. A team of former strangers gets to know each other as they work together and become more effective, as the culture fills up with knowledge about its members, their skills and potential contributions. The team does not become more and more effective indefinitely. There comes a time when they are all as well-known to each other as possible and could learn more outside. But the team rapidly gains in effectiveness during its early hours and some teams can be brilliantly innovative and develop cultures of unique excellence.

Teams go through stages, according to Bruce Tuckman. They go through a stage of initially FORMING, bottom left, then STORMING at each other (top left) as each member tries to make the definition of their joint mission as close to her/his qualifications as possible. Out of their strife emerges NORMING, agreed ways of discussing issues that elicits from everyone the best they have to give. They will be courteous, they will speak in turn civilly and they will try to achieve consensus. They need a thorough inventory of everyone's skills and knowledge. With the right norms in place they will start PERFORMING (top right) with growing effectiveness and solving the problems at hand. At this point they achieve peak effectiveness. They then begin ADJOURNING, see right of picture. This reminds us that teams are temporary. The members dissolve and form another team which starts the five processes all over again. It is this short life that makes teams exciting to be on, like a ship-board romance that will be over in four days so do it now! Groups that last long are called committees and we expect little of them. In contrast, team members do not delegate, they act and take responsibility for their actions. They identify with the team's mission, champion innovation and strive to excel.

SELF-FULFILLING PROPHECIES: THE IMPORTANCE OF THEORY Y

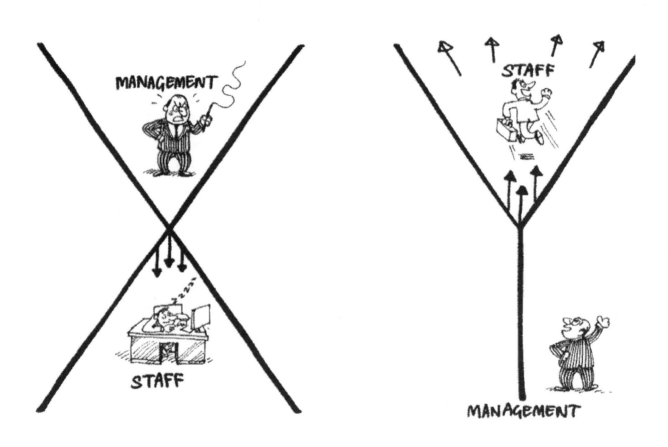

THE MANAGER'S BELIEFS ABOUT HIS/HER SUBORDINATES TEND TO COME TRUE. S/HE IS AT ONE END OF A SHARED RELATIONSHIP.

Throughout this book we have argued that was is missing in the way much of the West thinks of wealth creation, is the failure to grasp the importance of relationships. Hawthorne gave rise to the Human Relations movement. What Douglas McGregor of MIT learned from this experiment was that how the superior thinks about his subordinates and communicates with them, is all-important. The women subjects in the relay test room were treated as if they were associates of Harvard in an increasingly important and fascinating experiment, and for this reason they excelled. As productivity climbed, observers could not disguise their enthusiasm and the women did even better in response. McGregor called this Theory Y, see right image opposite. It is the belief that work is natural and enjoyable, that employees want to act responsibly and excel and that they seek to develop, learn, and win autonomy and self-direction. They are capable of dedication to organizational objectives. If the leader forms a relationship with them which confirms such beliefs, then these values fulfil themselves. It is the leader's responsibility where possible to establish such relationships. In contrast, Theory X, on the left of the illustration, believes that people dislike work and avoid responsibility and must therefore be motivated to accept it by money, by direction and, if need be, by coercive control. McGregor's book *The Human Side of the Enterprise* became very popular but was too often interpreted to suggest that leaders could "grow" their subordinates through sheer wish-fulfilment. The importance of particular relationships and warm friendships was lost amid a flood of universalized good-will applied to all employees regardless, a variation on positive thinking and a kind of spiritual technology. What we have are unique beings and every relationship is special and different. There are no formulae. To this issue we now turn.

᪖

THE PROCESS OF CONTINUOUS IMPROVEMENT: REWARDING THE TEAM

Planning and doing

Checking and acting to correct/improve

THE PROCESS OF CONTINUOUS IMPROVEMENT ALLOWS WORKERS IN QUALITY CIRCLES TO TAKE INITIATIVES AND MONITOR THEIR OWN SUCCESS. IF YOU WANT MORE CREATIVITY, REWARD THE WHOLE TEAM.

The US consultant W Edwards Deming is credited with inventing the process of Continuous Improvement in industry. Scorned by Detroit, he offered his services to the Japanese auto industry and was so successful that be became a national hero, despite being a foreigner. To this day a Deming Prize is offered for process innovation in Japanese industry. The Emperor even gave him a prize! Toyota, which he served much of his life, is worth more than the entire US auto industry. His method is set out opposite. Workers form quality circles and use their brains to PLAN an improvement. They then actually DO it. After this they CHECK whether or not it has raised output/reduced costs and if it has, they ACT to make the change permanent, only to PLAN again the next move. All this makes the day's work exciting and meaningful. When they work, they are testing a hypothesis, inquiring into a better way of working. Often money can be involved. If the plan has saved the company $1,000, 50% of this is awarded to the work team in a process called "gain sharing" or fate-sharing.

Fons Trompenaars, working at Shell's Amsterdam laboratories, established how much better it was to reward the team as a whole, rather than a particular individual. Let us follow the fortunes of the female worker opposite. The Plan is largely hers, as is the whole initiative, yet the money earned by the team for its gain is shared out equally. Is this fair? In the long-term, yes and it is also wise. The most creative person in a group is not universally popular. S/he often forces unwelcome changes on other people. If you give the whole team the gain, not just the instigator, the team will reward her socially. Being liked and respected by those among whom you work may be the strongest motivation known to employees. We can see her obvious pleasure at bottom left. Moreover, good ideas need to be fleshed out and actually implemented and she will have received help from colleagues. Were she to receive this money on her own, others could get envious. In any case she can now be promoted; as she is already the informal leader of the group this can be made official.

❧

HIGH CONTEXT IS A MEASURE OF RICH RELATIONSHIPS

The formal system, measured bench-marks. HQ on the phone.

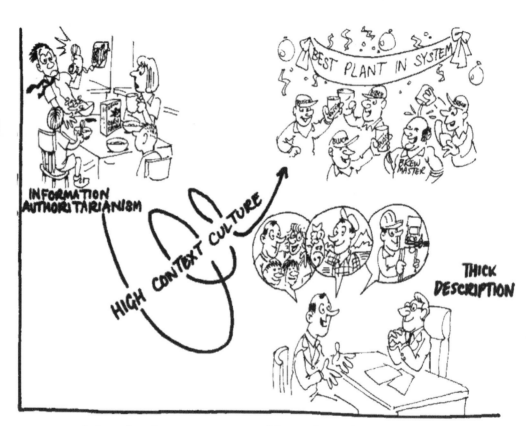

Interviewing persons and learning about them

THE RICHER THE RELATIONSHIPS, THE BETTER THE PLANT PERFORMED, GOING FROM THE WORST IN THE SYSTEM TO THE BEST.

This study is of interest because the change-agents deliberately emulated the effects of the Hawthorne Experiment, using interview protocols designed by Nevitt Sanford. The action-research programme for the Fairfield plant of the brewing company Anheuser Busch was conducted by the Meridian Group at the Wright Institute in Berkeley led by Royal Foote. Fairfield was the worst performing plant in the whole system. Since the HQ was in St. Louis operating in Central time, and Fairfield was in California operating in Pacific time, executives at Fairfield would be called at breakfast to be told that aluminium-wastage in their canning plant was up 4% and what did they plan to do about this? They felt such information was used to harass and shame them and morale was very low. The union threatened a strike because of it. The intervention by the researchers did not address any of these issues. It simply asked the head of the Fairfield plant to spend one day a month interviewing all his direct reports on any topic they wished to raise, even personal ones. There were to be no restrictions. Each direct report interviewed the persons reporting to him/her and so on down, with foremen interviewing hourly workers. There was no other advice or intervention given.

Two years after the start of interviews, Fairfield had climbed from the worst plant to the best by some distance. The more information we have about each other, the higher and thicker is the context of that culture. Since canning and shipping beer is not a very complex process and only the brew-master is really expert, we would not expect that knowing each other better would make much difference. Yet the shift in productivity and waste-reduction was dramatic. The union elected a more moderate leader and new methods of participation were instituted. The plant had once been the least profitable, even loss-making but its profits were now the best in the system. Fairfield was given information and only invited days later to say what action it had taken, but all these and other changes were captured by the interviews.

❦

B) LOW COST, HIGH QUANTITY PRODUCTS VS. QUALITY PREMIUM PRODUCTS?

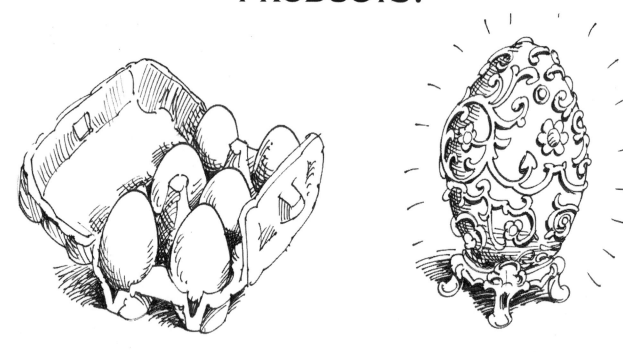

UNIVERSAL (HENS') EGGS   A PARTICULAR FABERGÉ EGG

MAKING MONEY FROM THE LOW COST OF YOUR COMMODITY OR FROM ITS PEERLESS, UNMATCHABLE QUALITY?

According to Michael Porter, there are two basic and alternative ways of proving profitable and of making money, and we should not confuse these. You can produce the cheapest product which appeals universally to those seeking to save expense, or you can supply a product of very particular distinction, whose premium quality no other can match, which gives you a virtual monopoly. We have illustrated this opposite with hens' eggs which, if cheap enough, will push competitors out of the market and a Fabergé Egg made for the Russian Royal Family by a French craftsman and extremely rare and precious. It follows the economic law that scarcity enhances value. Porter is adamant that these two appeals should not be mixed up or confused. Women rarely buy cheap cosmetics. They think of themselves as valuable, ("You're worth it!") and put expensive, high-margin products on their faces and skin. You cannot simultaneously save money and consider what you wear or use, as special. Porter cites the collapse of Laker Airlines when it ceased to emphasize cheapness and went after the business class market. He certainly has a point. These two appeals are very hard to combine and most companies do not succeed in doing so. However, some outstanding companies have succeeded in integrating both appeals successfully and we will be looking at two examples of this. In the meantime, Porter is quite right to suggest that this strategy is dangerous and we should be very careful of this. We turn to a popular British TV comedy called *Fawlty Towers* starring John Cleese, which shows the conflict between hiring a builder who is cheap and a builder who is extremely skilled and competent.

A HIGH-QUALITY COMPETENT BUILDER OR A CUT-PRICE COWBOY?

BEING INEXPENSIVE AND OF HIGH QUALITY OFTEN CLASHES AND ABOVE IS A SOURCE OF CONFLICT AND HUMOUR, BUT THIS IS NOT NECESSARILY SO.

ollisions between opposed values is a staple for many comedies. In this episode of *Fawlty Towers,* starring John Cleese as Basil Fawlty, he and his wife disagree about which builder to use; a reputable local called Mr. Stubbs who is highly professional but costs more, or a cheap cowboy and total incompetent called O'Reilly, who has already failed them in building a garden wall. When his wife goes out for the day, Basil seizes upon the opportunity to substitute O'Reilly for Mr. Stubbs and insists he build a door from reception into the dining hall of their hotel very quickly and cheaply before his wife returns. However, she returns at midday and finds O'Reilly there. He most unwisely tells her that he likes assertive women and she beats him with her umbrella! But when she leaves for the rest of the day Basil orders O'Reilly to complete his work, "We will show her!"

When Mr. Stubbs turns up the next day to do the alterations these are seemingly complete and Basil is smugly triumphant. "I take it you used a steel or jade lintel?" inquires Mr. Stubbs, "because that's a supporting wall. The whole hotel could fall in!" O'Reilly has failed yet again and the last scene in the programme is Basil marching down the road with a garden gnome with which to spur Mr. O'Reilly to better efforts. So, Michael Porter on the previous page has a point. Cheap offerings and premium offerings are different enough to lead to comedy and/or tragedy, had the hotel collapsed. However, human beings are more ingenious than we give them credit for. Two examples of integrated values follow and we show just how creative it is possible to be.

∽

LEXUS: LOW-COST FUSED WITH PREMIUM QUALITY

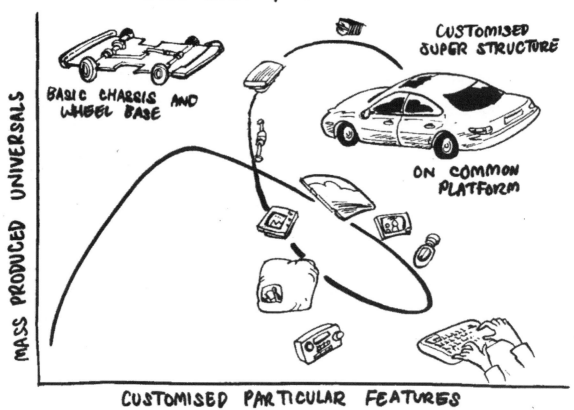

COST SAVING LUXURY

BASIC CHASSIS AND WHEEL BASE

CUSTOMISED SUPER STRUCTURE

ON COMMON PLATFORM

MASS PRODUCED UNIVERSALS

CUSTOMISED PARTICULAR FEATURES

CERTAIN HIDDEN PARTS OF THE VEHICLE CAN BE HIGHLY STANDARDISED AND COST-SAVING, WHILE THE PARTS YOU DO SEE CAN BE HIGHLY CUSTOMISED AND UNIQUE. QUANTITY IS ALWAYS OF A CERTAIN QUALITY.

The Toyota Lexus is our first example of how lowered costs can be fused with an expensive, luxury car, designed around the customer who buys it. After all, those who buy such cars know value-for-money when they see it. They might not be affluent otherwise. Wanting the best does not impede your judgment on value in general. In the case of the Toyota Lexus it has the same standardized chassis and wheelbase as other Toyotas. These are manufactured in bulk and much cost is saved thereby. However, unless you laid yourself under the car and looked up, you would not see what the Lexus had in common with cheaper brands. The part of the Lexus you can see is customized and consists of a super-structure imposed upon the car. You go into a show-room, pick a car approximate to what you want and enter all the special features you want your car to have into a computer. It will then be manufactured to your order and delivered in a few days. What we have, as the illustration shows, is a customized superstructure which makes the vehicle special, mounted upon a common base that saves money. The result is not cheap but nor is it extravagant and you are not paying for its diversity more than that diversity costs. Ronald Reagan forced upon the Japanese a limited quota of vehicles they could export to the USA but there was no limit on the value of each car which gave the Lexus its boost. It is clear from this illustration that having a premium product in no way lowers its economy as a vehicle. Compared to other luxury brands it delivers more via subtle standardization and volume savings. The choice of different features makes the car as different as the customer wants it to be, with, for example, virtual reality for the children in the back seat or a TV set that plays their favourite games.

DELL COMPUTERS WITH A STRATEGIC AND CUSTOMIZED PURPOSE

DELL COMPUTER: FROM PRODUCT TO SOLUTION

Low cost parts supplied by the million

COMPONENTS ORDERED EN MASSE

I.T ORGANISED TO SUPPORT STRATEGIC DIRECTION

STRATEGY PONDERED

Customizing clients' particular strategies

HARDWARE CONSISTS OF THE CHEAPEST RELIABLE COMPONENTS, WHILE THE SOFTWARE IS DESIGNED TO MONITOR AND DELIVER THE PARTICULAR STRATEGY WHICH THE CORPORATE CUSTOMER HAS CHOSEN.

Dell was a late-comer to the computer market. The retail outlets were full to choking with the computers of the then incumbents. Michael Dell had to do something different from the rest or he would make no impact. He decided to sell computers in quantity straight to companies, not through retail outlets. With one hundred and more ordered at a time, costs were kept low but more than that, he learned the purposes which the computers served strategically, and produced software customized to that end. For example, if you were an airline your software could predict how full your flight would be, based on early reservations and you could raise or lower your fares accordingly. In the picture opposite, we see that Dell orders computer parts by the million from suppliers which keeps costs very low. It does not manufacture at all but assembles parts en masse. Yet for the hundred or so computers ordered by any client, it installs the software with the special information the company needs to conduct its business. In short, the hardware is low cost and the software highly customized with the intention of supporting the company's strategic direction whatever that may be. Dell was greatly helped by the expansion of the Internet during its early years which assisted the customization process. Michael Dell also decided to buy back his shares from pubic ownership and get shareholders off his back. From early on, his suppliers had access to his levels of inventory for parts. Their job was to keep the inventory low but never let it run short, in other words, just in time. Every customer also had a complete online record of all past dealings and future plans. The supplier was a partner.

c) SOCIO-TECHNICAL LEARNING AS THE KEY TO DEVELOPMENT

Kolb's Learning Cycle.
contrasts:

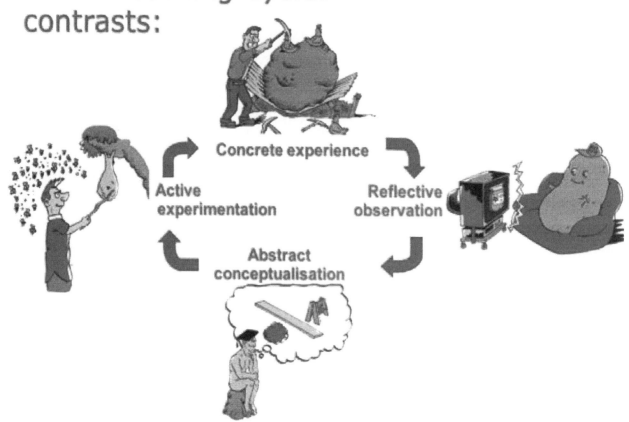

ALL LEARNING IS CIRCULAR AND NEEDS FEEDBACK FROM WHICH WE LEARN. IT MOVES FROM CONCRETE (TOP) TO ABSTRACT (BOTTOM) AND FROM ESTIMATING BEFOREHAND (LEFT) REFLECTING AFTERWARDS (RIGHT).

Opposite is an illustration of how people and organizations learn about running their enterprises. Any cycle can, of course, start at any one point, but for convenience we will start with experimentation on the left. This is followed by the experience (top) of the consequences of that experimentation. This experience may be onerous, even unpleasant; note the hornets. This is why it is sensible to reflect on your experience. Could you have worked in a more effective way? Can you improve your operations with hindsight? This leads you to abstract conceptualization of some of the problems you faced. Should the system be redesigned? Can you use physics, chemistry, engineering, blockchains and psychology to do better than before? Can you pin-point the problems and eliminate them? The learning of businesses often starts with active experimentation. They do not have the leisure or time like schools and universities do, of operating in a moratorium from busy-work. It can pay to be the first in the market even if your product is not yet perfect. Businesses often jump in at the deep end, get valuable experience and then improve as rapidly as possible. This obliges them to deal with myriad uncertainties, while schools and universities think first and then act. Many businesses find themselves acting experimentally and then thinking. Even if a certain amount of chaos results from your action, it is your chaos and you may operate in its midst better than your rivals and be the first to restore some semblance of order and extract rent from the situation. Disruptive innovation has recently been much discussed. Note that we are dealing with socio-technical learning. You learn about the technologies you are deploying and about its effect on customers and community. There is no technological change without social change and letting the former dominate can be folly.

RECONCILING ABSTRACT-CONCRETE, ACTIVE-REFLECTIVE

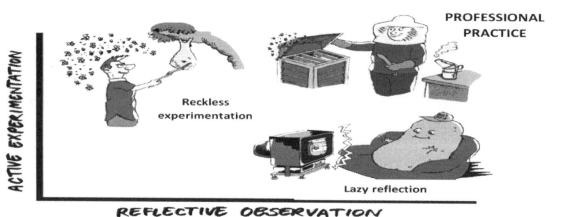

IF YOU WANT TO THINK RATIONALLY YOU NEED TO COMPARE WHAT ACTUALLY HAPPENED CONCRETELY WITH THE ABSTRACT CONCEPT YOU EMPLOYED. WHAT DID YOU THINK/HOPE WOULD HAPPEN WHEN YOU EXPERIMENTED AND, LOOKING BACK, WHAT IN FACT HAPPENED?

If we take the top and bottom of Kolb's Learning Cycle on the previous page, we see that values are not just joined in a circle but are reconciled and spiral upwards. In order to think abstractly, you must test your proposition via concrete experience of what you have been thinking about. The result is working smart, (not just hard). In order to actively experiment, you need to reflect on what occurred and learn from it. Note that experimentation without reflection and reflection without experimentation both fail, as does abstract thinking without concrete testing or vice versa. Values need to be integrated, to create professional practice (top-right) and the thoughtful leverage of working smart. Both Reckless experimentation (top left) and Lazy reflection (bottom right) are insufficient and unavailing, as are failing to work smart in the top illustration and only thinking without acting. Note that all these opposed values can increase in their intensity, provided they achieve balance and synergy. There is no limit to the riskiness of experimentation, provided it is deeply reflected upon. There is no limit to abstract thinking, provided it is checked up on by concrete experience. The integrity of these four lead to professional practice and working smart. Learning is a form of integrity.

D) CHANGE AND CONTINUITY: HOW TO FORGE A CORE COMPETENCE

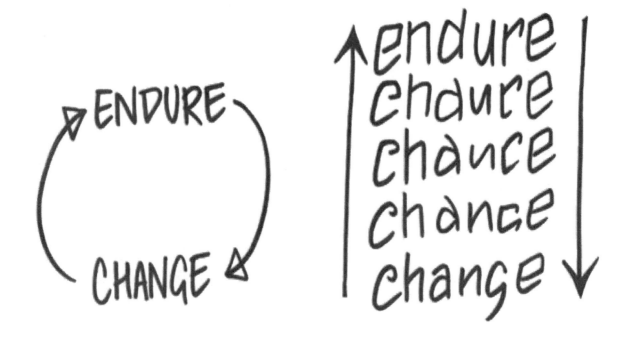

WE AS PERSONS CHANGE IN SOME RESPECTS WHILE REMAINING THE SAME AND FORGING AN IDENTITY. THE SAME APPLIES TO CORPORATIONS. THEY FORGE A CORE COMPETENCE OF LASTING CONVICTIONS/ COMMITMENTS WHILE RECONCEIVING THESE TO KEEP PACE WITH CHANGING WORLD EVENTS.

In order to succeed, a company must do something better than its rivals can do it. It must forge what Gary Hamel called a "core competence". It must develop an enduring body of skills and knowledge and must keep changing in order to serve a market also in flux. Moreover, as it combines skills with skills and ideas with ideas, it spurs innovation and in this sense changes what it has to offer over time. In order to change successfully, certain traits have to endure; you have to be even more professional, even more profitable, even more competent and even more helpful to more customers. Moreover, a company, like its individual members, has an identity. This is reflected in its good will, in its brand and in its reputation for fair dealing. In addition, it has to endure in some respects so that it can change in other respects; for example, it has to collect and classify ideas so it can use these to create new meanings. Note that the contrasting values circle around, as shown on the left, but also shift back and forth as shown on the right, with enduring melting into changing and changing melting into enduring. If the business environment is changing then the company has to change too for any bond to endure. We could have no clearer example of the dynamic, restless nature of values. We will be looking at the phenomenon of corner-stoning as practiced by Microsoft, placing one product on top of another in a succession of platforms. We will be looking at what you can do with a core competence in cultivating orchids and just how many changes can be wrung from this process in radically different contexts. Finally, we will be looking at selling not just the products of your manufacturing processes but these processes themselves, by installing these on your customers' premises.

CHANGE, CONTINUITY AND CORNER-STONING

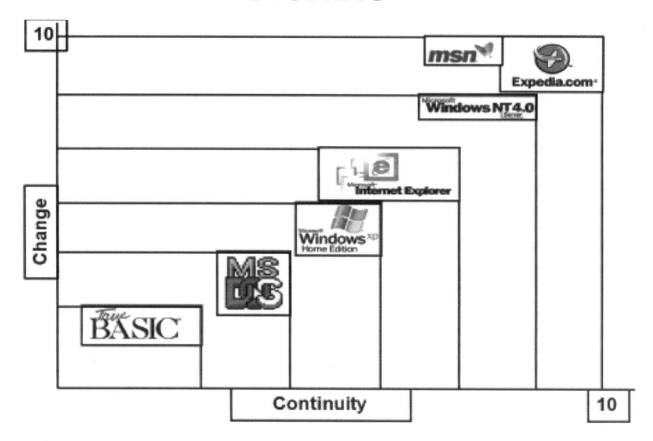

CORNER-STONING IS THE PROCESS OF MOUNTING ONE PRODUCT ON TOP OF THE PREVIOUS ONE AND SELLING ALL OF THEM, SO THAT THE INTERNET EXPLORER RE-SELLS WINDOWS WHICH RE-SELLS MS DOS AND TRUE BASIC. IT CHANGES AND CONTINUES, WHILE ACCUMULATING UNITS.

One way in which change with continuity manifests itself is through placing one product atop another like cornerstones. The older of the two products becomes a platform on which the newer is founded. Windows does not just place each successive product on top of the previous one, it makes its platforms available to entrepreneurs who can then mount their innovations upon its system. Corner-stoning was first named by Adrian Slywotsky, a highly original consultant at Mercer. The process is a powerful dynamic by which change and continuity are harnessed. True Basic at bottom left is a computer language, while MS-DOS uses that language and pays its dues. Windows is then mounted on the platform of MS-DOS and True Basic and the Internet Explorer uses Windows and the platforms below it. Windows NT. 4.0-10 and upwards brings out successive versions. Finally, msn.com and MSN Expedia.com are mounted on the five prior products-cum-platforms. Note that when you sell any one of these you create a change but this is founded upon an underlying continuity. You effectively re-sell and re-use the products underlying this change and thereby maintain your continuity, amounting to a monopoly. This is not just confined to electronics and software. Products increasingly come in generations with a parental platform beneath the new offspring. Innovation is becoming an industry but one that rapidly rises to dominate the field and shut out any rivals. On the other hand, allowing entrepreneurs to use your platforms and offering to co-venture in partnership with them as Philips of Eindhoven is doing, promises to open up opportunities. Philips has many unused patents which would-be entrepreneurs may choose to exploit.

CHANGE WORKS BEST WITH CONTINUITY OF DIRECTION

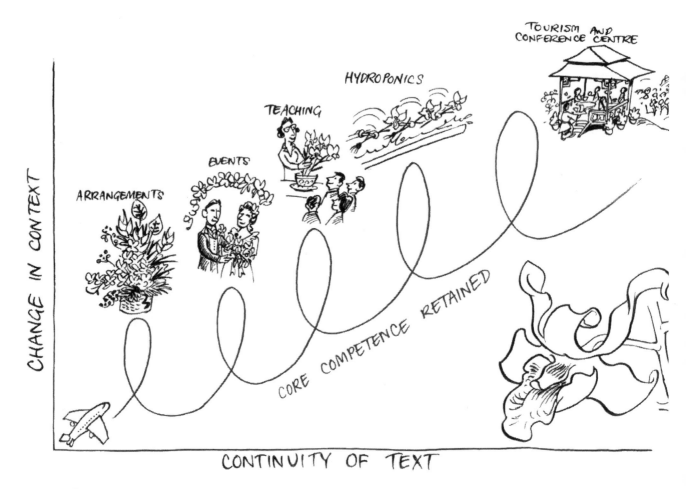

ORCHIDVILLE IN SINGAPORE STUCK TO ITS CORE COMPETENCE, GROWING ORCHIDS, BUT RANG THE CHANGES BY SELLING THESE IN NEW WAYS.

Orchidville is a Singaporean company founded by an ex-pig farmer with no college education. He was watching TV one evening when he was told that pig-farming was to be banned because of the smell. No one had bothered to tell him! He had more pigs than anyone else and asked for a month's stay which was unexpectedly granted. He used his month's grace to buy all pigs in the nation, slaughter and deep freeze them. He sold them to hotels and restaurants.

With his profits, he went into orchid farming, a hobby. He would freeze-dry orchids, fly them to Japan and sell them on the streets. But it was 1990 and Japan was entering recession. He faced disaster once more, so he approached top Singapore hotels. Would they like year-round displays of orchids, delivered, arranged and maintained? He had learned from his trips to Japan where flower arranging was a fine art. The hotels agreed. He next turned to those who visited the hotels, wedding planners, wine and glass suppliers, photographers, caterers etc. He would recommend the best of these if they would recommend his flowers. They agreed. Then he read that the government wanted to promote the life sciences. What about an orchid growing kit in every primary school classroom with the teacher explaining its growth? The government agreed. His next venture was into hydroponics with the help of a university. It is possible to grow orchids in a nurturant liquid that functions like soil and flows past the roots. If you wrap the roots in a bag of liquid you can send it abroad while still planted and it lasts longer. Singapore was the second largest orchid exporter in the world. Finally, many tourists would come to see his fields of waving flowers. He catered to them, offering drinks beneath thatched umbrellas, a dance floor, a shop and a conference centre. Note that all way through he maintained the CONTINUITY of orchids. He knew more than anyone else, yet he had wrung an amazing series of CHANGES, a new context for the development of his core competence. This story ends sadly, as the world market for orchids collapsed around 2015, but Orchidville was protected by its niche in the tourist industry and its other intelligent ventures.

E) COMPETING AT COOPERATING: THE ART OF CO-OPETITION

Empowering the larger ecosystem

Competing in any way you can get away with

Cooperating at risk to your own interests

WHAT COMPANIES COMPETE AT IS COOPERATING THE BEST WITH CUSTOMERS, WHO PREFER TO BE SERVED BY PEOPLE WHO ENJOY EACH OTHER. IT IS NOT POSSIBLE FOR A TEAM TO COMPETE WITHOUT COOPERATING.

The ideals of competing and cooperating have been historic enemies. The US and the UK are the traditional advocates of out-and-out competition, while the communists, socialists and liberal do-gooders advocate cooperation, liable, it is claimed, at any moment to become totalitarian! Very few values have become so dangerously polarized as these. In fact, neither value works in the absence of the other. The test of good cooperation within a company is that it makes the firm more competitive. The test of good competition between teams is that it binds you to your team more closely. What is needed is a fine interweaving of both values we shall call 'co-opetition'.

The problem with competition as an ideal is that it becomes promiscuous and predators beat up on the weakest, usually customers. The problem with cooperation as an ideal is that it can be used to stifle dissent and disagreement and is too open to being exploited, see bottom right of picture. You have to combine the two values, but this is easily done. For example, you can compete to come up with good ideas, pick the winners and then cooperate to make the best ideas viable. You can give an important problem to several teams and have them cooperate internally to win externally. You can have ventures compete and then learn cooperatively from the best features of each effort. We will be looking at how IBM came to compete in a very different way and how Motorola staged competitions in how well teams had served customers, and how very macho and competitive truck drivers came to cooperate with the highways' authority of California on safety issues. It is more and more true that competition is taking place between whole industrial eco-systems, not companies alone, but their supply-chains, partners and customers. Competing within these eco-systems can be sub-optimal. Where such systems consist of scores of shareholder groups all trying to maximise their incomes, the competition may be excessive and the cooperation too little.

⚘

How competition at IBM helped to spur cooperation and raise sales

ALWAYS ASK WHAT IT IS THAT YOU ARE COMPETING AT. IF YOU ARE COMPETING TO "LEARN FROM CUSTOMERS" THEN THE WINNER SHARES THIS WITH ALL OTHER CONTESTANTS AND EVERYONE LEARNS.

C H-T interviewed Tim Gallwey some years ago. He is a consultant and author of *The Hidden Game of Tennis* and other works. This account comes from an interview he gave us about engaging IBM and its sales-force. IBM was proud and enthusiastic about its bi-annual sales contest in which its top sales person received a free holiday for self and family in Acapulco. Yet there were problems IBM wanted Tim to remedy. The same one or two sales persons were winning year after year. They never let on how they did it, lest someone beat them next time. Customers were complaining of hard-sell tactics and suspected (rightly) that the sales person had her/his own agenda. Newly trained employees were quitting in despair of getting near the contest winners. There were stress-related symptoms among the sales force. Tim had been warned privately not to recommend any abandonment of the sales contest. It was an honoured tradition. The situation he found is top left of the illustration opposite, "Hard sell all the way". Winning ways were top secret.

What Tim recommended was most ingenious and kept the sales contest in place while changing what it was about. In future he commended the prize should be given to the sales person who had learned most from customers during the previous six months. This could only be judged by presenting this information to the conference. The conference would vote on the most valuable presentation, see top right. All this changed the conduct of the sales force. In order to win the contest, it had to listen to what the customer said, note it down (bottom right) and pass it on. The top sales persons still won most of the time but the remainder improved markedly and the scores were much closer than before. Overall sales rose by over 20%. It is incredibly more effective to listen and learn from the customer than to try and pressure him into buying.

COMPETING AT TOTAL CUSTOMER SATISFACTION AT MOTOROLA

Cooperating within teams to help customers

WHERE TEAMS COMPETE TO SERVE CUSTOMERS, THE INTERNAL COOPERATION OF TEAM MEMBERS IS VITAL TO BEING COMPETITIVE.

This illustration comes from the hey-day of Motorola in the 1990s when it instituted a world-wide contest in 'TCM', total customer satisfaction. Some 800 sales teams from all the countries in which the company operated could compete in the quality of their work retrospectively. Typical of team-work was installing up-to-date communications equipment in air ambulances or connecting Israeli tanks with support units on the battlefield. A team that believes it has done superlative work first competes with other teams within its region. This proved so popular in Singapore and Malaysia that teams from other companies were allowed to join in and the government sponsored the contest locally. This was followed by a contest between regions of Motorola with the dozen or so finalists coming to the Paul Galvin Theatre at Schaumburg, Illinois. They competed by going up on the stage, dramatizing what they did for the customer, showing the results and featuring the customer's gratitude and enhanced performance. The finalists were all honoured; many of them were in the USA for the first time and all taken very seriously by Motorola University which gathers examples of best practice from the whole world and uses these to educate. The presentations make fine educational material. The illustration opposite shows that Competing can be taken too far with unfair advantage being gained. Cooperating can deteriorate into cosy collusion with outsiders excluded. What keeps a company excelling is cooperation within teams and between teams and customers, followed by competing in the results of such exercises, which identifies which of these practices are best. A 36% improvement in a customer's productivity can be celebrated (top right). East Asian teams did especially well. No one had invited them to show off before! Note that cooperation at one level facilitates competition at a higher level. How well you have cooperated internally becomes a function of how well you compete externally. Nations in Asia with a communitarian cultural ethic have a competitive advantage over the West.

How Macho truck-drivers became 'Knights of the road'

Competing with the highway patrol and safety regulations

Cooperating with company and state authorities on safety

CB COWBOYS

...CAN INCINERATE A SMALL VILLAGE

KNIGHTS OF THE ROAD

"BE MORE CAREFUL, BOYS"

A really tough guy comes to the rescue of others.

A California-based oil company faced a serious problem with its tanker truck drivers. This is one of the highest paid jobs open to working class people and the drivers were preponderantly male with a macho culture of tough and lonely independence, generally absent from their homes. The company worried because a crashed tanker can be lethal and can potentially incinerate a small village (see middle of illustration), where gasoline spills on the road, runs down into cellars and ignites pilot lights. If a tanker is in a multi-vehicle pile-up it can set fire to the resulting heap. But perhaps most worrying is that drivers use their CB radios to warn each other of speed-traps (see top left) and generally compete against the California Highway Patrol, attempting to out-wit any plan to make them slow down. High speeds raised a driver's productivity. Earnest advice to 'be more careful boys' (see bottom right) was unavailing.

To solve this problem, the company created a Knights of the Road programme which re-wrote the drivers' job description. Their mission was to make Californian highways safer and success in doing this would be celebrated. Like knights of old, they would come to the rescue of the travelling public. Their CB radios gave them the opportunity to warn the Highway Patrol of rock-slides, broken-down vehicles and other hazards. They would be rewarded for reporting these and honoured if lives were saved thereby. It turned out that the drivers were worried about safety too – several had written wills. What upset them most were the ramps for entering the highway. Several of these were so short that tankers were forced to enter the highway at around 45 mph when ongoing traffic was travelling at 60 mph or more. A fully loaded tanker with the accelerator flat down could not achieve a sufficiently high speed to slip into traffic safely. They were allowed to borrow film equipment from the company and film such hazards. Once a year they gave a presentation to the State Road Safety Commission and several of their recommendations were implemented; essentially, they became consultants on road safety. The programme was extremely successful and the number of unsafe acts dropped sharply. They were still 'competing' with the Highway Patrol but now in a more constructive way!

RULES AND EXCEPTIONS:
AUSTRALIA VS. JAPAN

THE JAPANESE ASKED AUSTRALIAN SUGAR GROWERS TO RE-NEGOTIATE THE CONTRACT WHEN THE WORLD PRICE OF SUGAR FELL.

Two values that cause much conflict but are reconcilable by intelligent systems, are rules with ambitions to be universal, and particular exceptions to such rules. Each side of such conflicts regards itself as moral and the opposing side as ethically deficient. In the 1970s there was a long bitter and very public row between Australian sugar growers and the Japanese confectionery industry. The latter had just signed a contract committing it to buy Australian sugar long-term at $10 a ton, below market price. The Australians would get assured sales for an extended period, the Japanese would get a break on the price paid. There was just one problem. Hardly was the ink dry than the world price of sugar collapsed. The Japanese found themselves obligated to buy sugar at $5 a ton above the world market price. They protested that these events were exceptional. No one had predicted such a fall in the world price and they asked to renegotiate. But the Australians were hardly in the mood to do so. They had taken a big hit as it was. "Is this signature worth the paper it is written on?" they demanded to know. What was the point of negotiating and contracting if one was not to honour the terms? Suppose the world price had risen? Would the Japanese want to re-negotiate then? The price collapse was serious enough for the growers, what was proposed would add to it! The Japanese pointed out that if they had to pay more than the world price their whole industry would suffer a serious disadvantage compared to other nations. If their industry suffered so would the Australian growers. Were they not partners in this misfortune? Should they not help each other? Surely the Australians could not want their customer to suffer? What was important was that both reach a satisfactory agreement. The larger truth is that exceptions improve rules. After many years of bitter recrimination, a solution was found. The Japanese would get their sugar for $5 dollars below the market price, whatever the market price was at the time. Both values had been served. The agreement was firm yet flexible. Our classes take 3 minutes to solve this problem. It took Australia and Japan 8 years!

Samsung as an exception to the rules: Was our copyright infringed?

Exceptional relationship with Samsung

Should intellectual property come before human relationships?

The Dutch author of this book made a presentation to Samsung at the end of the 1980s and gave them a copy of our book *Riding the Waves of Culture* in English. He was pleased but puzzled to receive a letter from them to say that they had translated his book into Korean and distributed many copies to their employees who found it invaluable. The publisher of the book was also puzzled but seriously displeased. The copyright had been flagrantly infringed by a major company. For the Netherlands and much of the West, rules come before exceptions. For a family dynasty the size of Samsung, they had a special relationship with us and rules could in time catch up. Samsung would not do that today. The West is more powerful in imposing its "rules first" doctrine, but at that time we decided to go along with Samsung's view of the matter. After all, our book explained that for much of SE Asia relations were more important than rules. We could have sued them (top left) and won a Pyrrhic victory, which would have foregone any future consulting opportunity with Samsung. We could have invited them to purloin more of our books (bottom right). We could have compromised at 5/5 and annoyed everyone. Instead, we thanked Samsung and asked them if they knew any Korean publishers. They not only knew them but owned them! The book was published and, thanks to Samsung's endorsement, sold very well. Even our publisher was pleased. The translation turned out to be excellent. Countries where exceptional relationships are regarded as more important than rules are more flexible and adaptable in their business dealings and arrive more easily at agreements where both sides win, as they did in this case. Such countries are growing faster economically. East Asia has many fewer lawyers per head of population. We might consider learning and spend less time beating up on each other in courts of law.

Southwest Airlines, rules, exceptions and humour

Rules, broken in error

Exceptional Customer Service, used to correct

The passenger who sat down on a dried ginger root.

The incident illustrated opposite occurred with Southwest Airlines and is written up in *Nuts: Southwest Airlines' Crazy Recipe for Business and Personal Success* by Kevin and Jackie Freiberg. The company was brilliantly led by Herb Kelleher and has succeeded despite the chronic failure of most other US airlines, who are filing for bankruptcy to renege on its promises to staff and contractors. The airline is rightly famous for its record fast turn-around time between the plane arriving and departing. It means the plane must be cleaned and re-stocked very quickly with even pilots helping. But with all this haste there are occasional slip-ups. A dried ginger root was erroneously left on a passenger seat and the next occupant sat down upon it. It penetrated his jeans and imparted some heat. The plane was taxying for take-off when he jumped up and demanded to visit the toilet. The stewardess could not permit this but delivered relief in the form of an ice-pack on which he sat until the plane had gained sufficient height to let him rise. Amongst some merriment in the in-house journal, she was congratulated for reconciling the Rules (opposite) with Exceptional Customer Service. The rules are there for customer safety but that must not stop staff from using their wits to solve problems not anticipated by the rule-book. What raises an airline above all others are acts of kindness and mercy we did not expect, delivered by those with presence of mind who care for those they serve. The whole incident and reaction to it also illustrates that human beings make errors but where these are admitted and shared, they are quickly corrected and the airline learns from this that it should improve its service continuously. All this is greatly enhanced if you can laugh at the situation and find fun in serving others.

g) The two Gods of Time: Chronos and Kairos

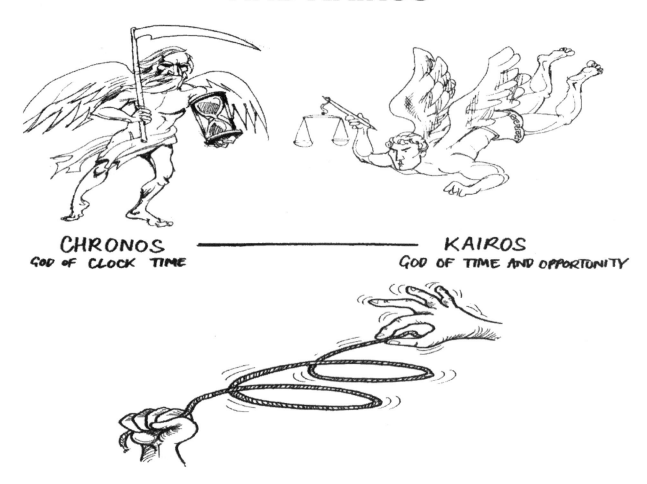

CHRONOS
GOD OF CLOCK TIME

KAIROS
GOD OF TIME AND OPPORTUNITY

SHOULD WE THINK OF TIME AS A SEQUENCE OR AS SYNCHRONISATION?

There were two gods of time in the view of Ancient Greece. There was Chronos, with his scythe and his hour glass who reaps us when our time is up. He was the god of *sequential* time, of time as an arrow or passing vehicle. And there is Kairos with his scales balanced on a razor blade who was god of *time and opportunity,* of "seize the time", of the "idea whose time has come." This is synchronous time, as in "synchronize your watches". We have axioms that invoke both concepts. "Time is money... Procrastination is the thief of time... Never put off to tomorrow what you can do today...Time like an ever-rolling stream bears all its sons away...Time and tide wait for no man..." These are all axioms of sequential time. But there are also axioms of synchronous time. "What goes around comes around... Many happy returns of the day... There is a tide in the affairs of men that taken in the flood leads on to fortune..."

Sequential time is a line with a definite direction. Synchronous time is a circle, like the two kinds of watches, one digital, one circular. These two concepts of time are reconciled by the helix opposite that circles around but has a forward trajectory. Time marches on but it also spins. We cycle developmentally upwards towards higher levels on integration. We will be examining Time and Motion Studies, how factories are designed in having parts reach the central assembly line "just in time" to produce many customized vehicles coming off the production line in great diversity. You make money by doing things quickly but you also make money by synchronizing operations. The fusion is the ever-faster dance.

∽რ

Time & Motion (American) or Just-in-time (Japanese)?

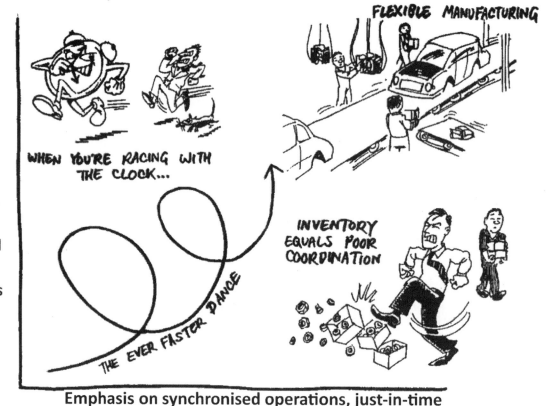

Emphasis on sequential speed of operations

FLEXIBLE MANUFACTURING

WHEN YOU'RE RACING WITH THE CLOCK...

INVENTORY EQUALS POOR COORDINATION

THE EVER FASTER DANCE

Emphasis on synchronised operations, just-in-time

PILES OF IN-PROCESS INVENTORY WERE A SURE SIGN OF POOR SYNCHRONISATION OF WORK, WHICH TAICHI OHNO USED TO KICK AT WHENEVER HE CAUGHT SIGHT OF IT.

The two different concepts of time appeal in varying degrees to different cultures. The USA began using time in a major way with its Time and Motion Studies inaugurated by Frederick Winslow Taylor. The assembly line moved fast in a straight line and workers were expected to keep up with it. This process was satirized in *The Pyjama Game,* a Broadway musical, when the employees sang:

When you're racing with the clock/The second hand does not understand
That your back may break/And your fingers ache/And your constitution isn't made of rock.

Taylor believed that the faster people moved, the more time and money would be saved and that people must strive to fulfil the potential of improving technology. There were several downsides. Work was grossly simplified so that skills atrophied, workers were exhausted and people were mere means to maximum machine utilization. That said, there were impressive gains in productivity. The Japanese studied Taylor with great respect but added a concept of their own, time as coordination between operations, or just-in-time. Operations could be done in parallel and then integrated. Parts could rendezvous with a vehicle in the process of assembly and fifty customized cars, all different, would come off the end of the assembly line. One important way of estimating how well this was being done was the level of in-process inventory. If work is poorly coordinated then parts completed by worker A will pile up between him/her and worker B. But if they get their rhythm right the piles will disappear. The head of Toyota was famous for kicking any piles of inventory he found between work spaces, see bottom right. It is Flexible Manufacturing that reconciles these two concepts of time in an Ever-Faster Dance, which is both quick and well-coordinated. Just-in-time keeps inventories low and carrying costs minimal. Suppliers deliver just before parts run out. Inventory levels are on-line and suppliers maintain them accordingly.

❧

TEAMS SOLVING PROBLEMS OVER TIME

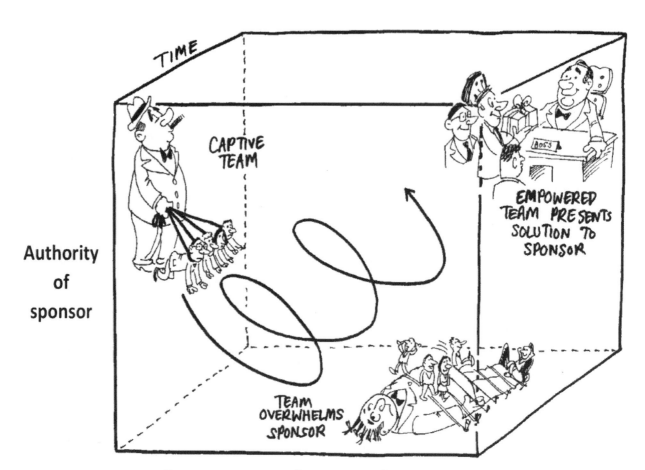

Empowerment of sponsored team

HOW AUTHORITY TO SOLVE PROBLEMS CAN BE DELEGATED BY LEADERS TO TEAMS WHO REPORT BACK WITH RECOMMENDATIONS.

Thus far we have used many dual axes to illustrate how values are optimally combined, yet time plays a part in all of these, because values are developed over time by doing things sequentially or synchronously. Here we visualize a cube with time as the third dimension. In the picture opposite a senior manager has sponsored a team to solve a recurring problem in the organization or launch a new venture. Membership is matched to the challenge faced and the team meets for a period of time. Essentially the solution has been delegated to some of those who have experienced the problems to be overcome and so know about these. Given the salaries paid to experts, this is an expensive process. Some sponsors worry that the team won't be up to the job and they seed it with their spies and cronies who report back to the sponsor as to what is likely to emerge (see top left). This is self-defeating. If the sponsor knows the answer, then he does not need a team! What he fears is at bottom right, that the team will get excited over a hare-brained scheme and tie him down to some crazy proposal. He will lose his authority and be blamed for wasting money. What he needs to do is choose the members wisely, explain what any solution must accomplish, give them sufficient resources and leave them alone to get on with it. They may seek guidance from him about the approach they are taking but he lets them empower themselves and does not interfere. At top right they restore his authority and empower themselves by presenting their solution. Jack Welch, in his latter days at GE, sponsored many scores of work-out groups on problems and opportunities facing the organization. He implemented close to 80% of their solutions unchanged. This process helps to build leaders of the future ready to accept responsibility.

H) CAN A CONFIDENT LEADER BE A HUMBLE SERVANT?

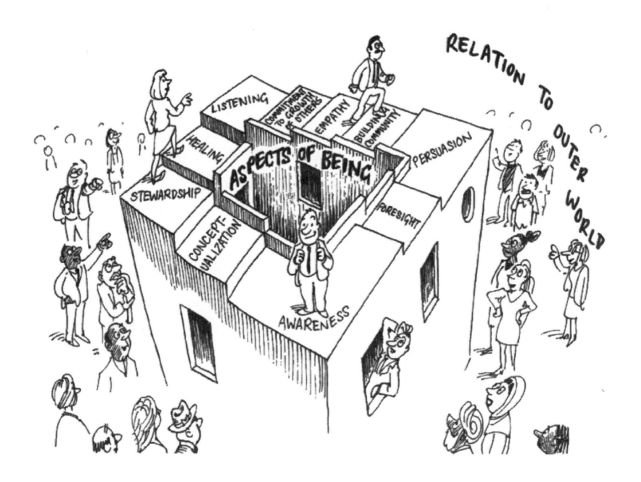

THE MORE HUMBLY AND FAITHFULLY YOU
SERVE A CAUSE GREATER THAN YOURSELF,
THE MORE THAT CAUSE WILL ELEVATE YOU.

Robert Greenleaf has celebrated the idea of the Servant Leader. The example of such a person was portrayed in the novel *Journey to the East* by the German writer Hermann Hesse. A group of brilliant historical characters magically re-incarnated, set out on a journey of self-discovery as a group of seemingly enlightened seekers. They are sustained on their journey by a servant on whom they learn to count. He is always there to help them, while claiming no wisdom or distinction. When the servant mysteriously vanishes, the pilgrims search in vain and then start to fall out with one another. Without service nothing works. The spiritual journey fragments into chaos. He is eventually traced by the story teller and turns out to have been the greatest among them. The more humbly and faithfully you serve a cause greater than yourself, the more it will elevate you.

Greenleaf was a senior telephone executive in a period when AT&T was expanding exponentially. Calls were getting ever cheaper, with more people reachable, an early example of the Net Effect, where one person joined to 100, creates 100 more relationships. He argued that the kind of service epitomized by his company was the underlying legitimation of effective leadership. You humbly serve an edifice, greater than you, and it is the edifice that raises you up and gives you the confidence to lead. If we look at the staircase opposite it is ascending and descending, to climb is to serve. The values inscribed on the various steps are those suggested by Greenleaf himself. You could direct people because you had listened. You could persuade so well because you had empathy. Your self-awareness enabled you to build community. Your humility before the edifice you were building was genuine. You were its servant, yet the edifice itself raised you up as the leader of an important development that brought benefits to the world outside. It was this edifice that made you confident of the benefits you could bestow. It was the power of this edifice to help people which made you grateful and humble to serve it.

How humble service can elevate you to the top

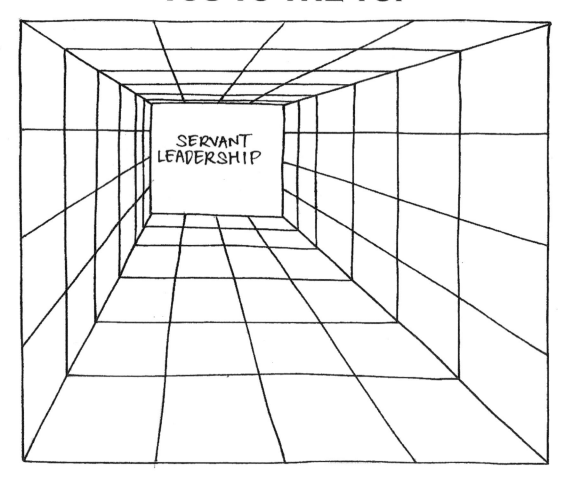

Finally, Nelson Mandela's jailors and prosecutors had to accept his authority over the whole nation, not just them.

The image opposite is ambiguous in the extreme. Is the servant leader at the bottom of a deep shaft or at the apex of a steep pyramid? Is s/he a tower of strength before the world or someone with deep insight and sympathy with the human condition, willing to serve it obediently? Surely these two sets of values are contradictory and hence nonsense? You cannot have it both ways. But you *can* have it both ways if what you lead is different from whom you serve. What happens with great leaders like Mahatma Gandhi, Martin Luther King, Nelson Mandela and others is that you humbly serve the Cause, the Movement, the Edifice, the Law, the Company, the Nation, even the World, while rising to lead the very institutions and social movements you have served so well. Vis-à-vis the organization you are serving, you are dedicated, hard-working, humble, unselfish, healing and busy developing others. Vis-à-vis the Movement you head you are confident, proud-to-serve, full of conviction, undaunted, fearless and greatly aspire. Servant Leaders frequently obey the law; Gandhi was a barrister serving the law. This is why he frequently went to jail and offered no resistance to arrest. This is why he was polite to judges and the court and accepted the sentences they imposed upon him. He was a subject of the crown. Yet that did not stop him explaining patiently and politely that the law was wrong and had been imposed on India by an alien colonial power intent on being a master in a house not its own. Gandhi himself was an expert on rights not applicable to himself! The longer Mandela languished in prison and in seeming disgrace, the more popular and powerful he became! Finally, his jailors and prosecutors were forced to accept his authority over not just them, but the whole land.

A TRIUMPH OF SELF-EFFACEMENT: WRETCHED BUREAUCRAT LEARNS TO LIVE

THE FILM IS SILENT THEN A SLOW SMILE SPREADS ACROSS HIS FACE. HE IS UNDAUNTED. THIS LAST ACT IS HIS LIFE AND HIS LEGACY.

Watanabe is an ageing, Japanese provincial bureaucrat whose nick-name in the office is "the Mummy", because he has been all but dead for years. The story *Ikiru*, (To Live), is from a film by the same name by Akira Kurosawa. Some mothers present Watanabe with a petition for a playground for their children. He tosses it aside - it will require six departments to agree, quite impossible. That evening he goes to the doctor and another patient who has identical symptoms to his, warns him the doctors will lie to him. They will say that any cancer is an ulcer. They do not want to be bothered. Minutes later the lie is told and the shadow of death passes across him (bottom left). He tries to go to parties to enjoy himself (top left) but cannot stop crying. Back in the office he retrieves the petition from where he threw it. He will get that playground built in the time he has left! There is a semi-feudal tradition in Japan that if you ask for something humbly enough and persistently enough, not just losing face but offering to trample on it, then the person petitioned must yield, a variation on *noblesse oblige*. You surrender status in exchange for what you want. Watanabe begs and cringes before department after department and each gives way rather see a senior employee abase himself even more. Even the mayor changes his mind. A group of gangsters who want to build a bar on the same ground come into his office and threaten his life. The film is silent for over thirty seconds then a smile spreads across his face. He is undaunted! His mortality is his life. He has not the time to get angry. The last we see of him is seated on a child's swing in the finished playground, humming a happy song. It is late at night and snowing. He is found in the morning frozen to death, surrounded by his legacy. Where he died children will henceforth play. This was Abe Maslow's favourite film. Those inquiring into his famous concept of self-actualization were referred to it.

⁂

SERVING THE INFINITE GAME, NOT THE FINITE GAME

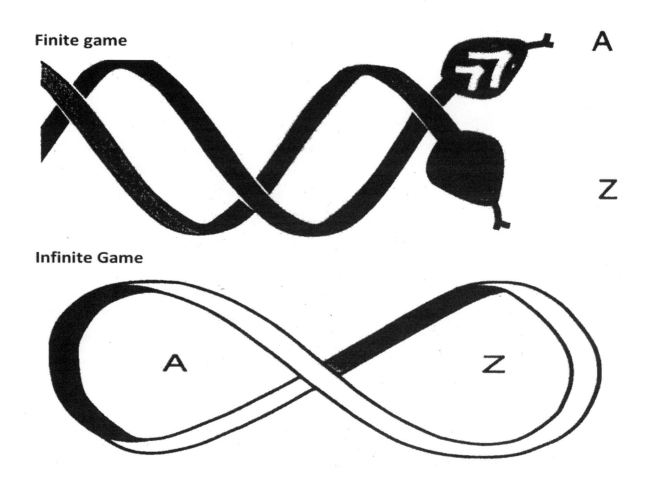

Finite game

A

Z

Infinite Game

A

Z

THE FINITE GAME IS WINNING SO OTHERS MUST LOSE.
THE INFINITE GAME DISTILS THE WISDOM OF WINNING
PLAYS AND PASSES THESE ON TO ALL PLAYERS SO THEY
LEARN TO MASTER THE ART OF WEALTH CREATION.

At the top is the Finite Game of businesses winning and losing against each other. In this world you are a winner and a leader, or a loser and a servant and there is nothing in between. You gobble up the resources of the loser you defeat. But the Servant Leader extols the Infinite Game, the martial art which is the art of service through leadership itself.   It discovers, through study, the reasons games were won by one contestant rather than the other. The two kinds of game contrast as follows:

Finite Game	*Infinite game*
The aim is to win	The aim is to improve the game
The fittest survive	The game evolves
Winners exclude losers	Winners teach losers better plays
Winner takes all	Winnings widely shared
Aims are identical and short-term	Aims are diverse and long-term
Rules fixed in advance	Rules changed by agreement
Rules resemble debating contest	Rules resemble grammar of original utterances
Contests existing markets	Grows new markets

The Servant Leader creates and serves the Infinite Game in the hope of improving Best Practice and serving everyone in the industry, the nation and the world. This distinction is by James P Carse. It is, among things, a search for excellence, a way of putting wealth creation above the fray. It conceives of creating value as a "game", capable of infinite improvement over time, an art form to be passed down the generations from master to master. It puts The Way, as in Chinese philosophy, above all contenders and all contention. It marries competition to harmony and is the martial art of peaceful conduct...

❧

1) UNDERSTANDING THAT WHOLES ARE MORE THAN THEIR PARTS

Parts ————————————————————— Wholes

"MAY GOD US KEEP FROM SINGLE VISION AND FROM NEWTON'S SLEEP." WILLIAM BLAKE

William Blake was very critical of Sir Isaac Newton and what he regarded as his analytical observations of very small parts of whole natural phenomena. "May God us keep from single vision and from Newton's sleep," he wrote to a friend. In the design opposite taken from Blake, Newton is depicted as hunched over himself calculating with a pair of dividers while sitting on a rock covered in the beauteous forms of natural phenomena. He is totally obsessed by the pin-point calculations before him. Time and again in this book we have seen that the whole is greater, more wealth-creating, more value-added than its various constituents and even the sum of these. The whole has greater meaning, is more complex, is more innovative and has emergent properties not present in the parts that went into it. The clue to being creative is to take a broader, more inclusive view, not just in the box, but out of it. Not unsurprisingly, the relationships of parts to wholes holds several clues as to how wealth is created and those who best manage the parts-whole relationship are notably more successful. We will be looking at IKEA and its sale of furniture, which it cleverly sells in flat-packs, to be assembled by the customer back home, and how it sells entire, whole room designs rather than alternative sticks of furniture. Finally, what part do cheap standardized modules play in whole original designs?

৯১

PARTS AND WHOLES: HOW IKEA DOES IT

Whole, elegantly designed living spaces

SOPHISTICATED SWEDISH DESIGN

SPECIFIC PIECES WITHIN DIFFUSE WHOLES

DISPLAY ROOM ABOVE

WAREHOUSE WITH SPECIFIC PIECES

Inexpensive parts stored in flat packs

WHAT IKEA REALLY SELLS ARE WELL-DESIGNED LIVING SPACES; WEALTH LIES WITHIN THE WHOLE, AESTHETIC PATTERN OF THE HABITAT.

IKEA, the Swedish furniture retailer, has a business model that fits parts into wholes in a finely fitting pattern. It invented the flat-pack, the large, shallow boxes in which all the parts of say, a table, are packed in such a way as to take up as little room as possible. This saves money in both delivery and storage (see lower right of illustration). Thanks to the flat-pack many customers can pick up what they have ordered from the ground floor warehouse and fit it into their vehicles, saving on delivery costs. But what IKEA sells are not sticks of furniture but well-lit and well-designed living spaces, or ideal kitchens, bathrooms, living rooms, bedrooms and studies. What this means is that someone in search of a chair for their study might decide to remodel their entire study when they see what IKEA's design is for such a room. In short, what is sold is the entire room design rather than the pieces within it. Perhaps the lighting makes the real difference, or the table for the PC and peripherals arranged around it. It is the optimal organization of living spaces that IKEA offers. Space is saved by asking the customer to assemble the furniture at home. The company recently acquired Task Rabbit so people adept at assembling IKEA's furniture could do so quickly and easily for customers of lesser dexterity. Part of IKEA's economy comes from customers doing the work. If you ask for help in the store, staff will show you where the information you need is located so you need not ask them again. The company's skill lies in simple, frugal products, tastefully arranged in wholes comprising idealized living-spaces which are more attractive together as a system than they are apart. Much of what they sell is wood and glass and neither are by themselves expensive. It is how they are combined that creates wealth.

KNOWLEDGE IS WHOLE, DATA ARE BUT PARTS

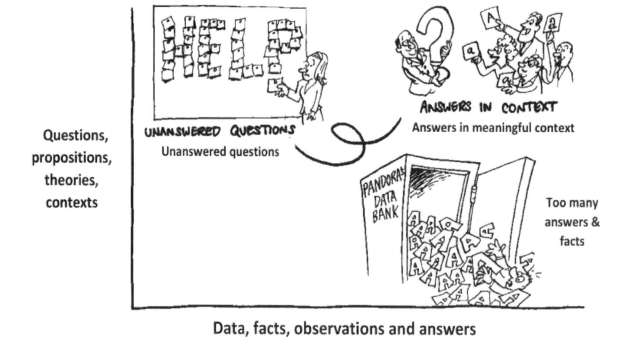

Questions, propositions, theories, contexts

UNANSWERED QUESTIONS
Unanswered questions

ANSWERS IN CONTEXT
Answers in meaningful context

Too many answers & facts

Data, facts, observations and answers

KNOWLEDGE SHOULD NOT BE CONFUSED WITH DATA OR FACTS. IT ANSWERS QUESTIONS AND MAKES SHARED MEANINGS OUT OF DIALOGUE WITH EMPLOYEES

Knowledge should not be confused with data, observations, facts and details. In the age of the Internet there are many more of these than we can possibly process. In Pandora's data bank there are too many answers and observations (bottom right). They tumble out and inundate us. We face a torrent of events and statistics and do not know what to make of these. We need to process such information and turn it into knowledge but we often do not know how. Every text needs a context. Without a question essential to survival, answers do not make sense. Data may or may not be relevant to us. What we need are propositions. Do people want this product or service? Can we supply it now and in the future? What value dilemmas are we facing and how can we reconcile these? Data, information and answers are parts. Questions, propositions and contexts seek wholes. We can only steer a company or a nation strategically and intelligently if we seek answers to questions, confirmation or otherwise for propositions, and solutions to the dilemmas we face. The woman asking for help (top left) has too many unanswered questions. The data bank (bottom right) has too many answers that no one wants to know. Between them they do not constitute knowledge. They are meaningless in the sense of being disconnected. What is required for knowledge to steer an organization is that leaders pose questions, issue challenges, state propositions and provide the context to which employees go out and find the answers, test propositions, try to meet challenges and report these to their leaders. Without some theory, even if mistaken, the data make no sense. They either uphold the assumptions being made or they do not. What is required is a dialogue between those asking questions and those discovering answers. Each has part of what both need to know, so only mutual respect and patient listening will do. Knowledge is a whole system of explanation and nothing else will do. We need meaningful purposes to which answers contribute.

CREATING WHOLES OUT OF CHEAP STANDARDIZED MODULES

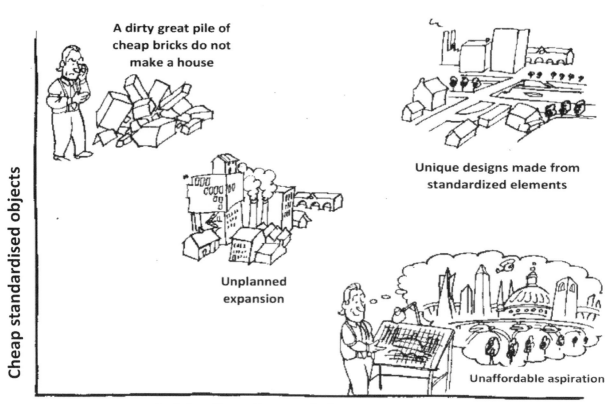

A dirty great pile of cheap bricks do not make a house

Unique designs made from standardized elements

Unplanned expansion

Unaffordable aspiration

Cheap standardised objects

Originality of overall design

WHAT IS NEEDED IS A HIGHLY ORIGINAL DESIGN MADE OUT OF STANDARD PARTS/MODULES. IT IS THE RELATIONSHIP AMONG THE VALUES THAT COUNTS.

The whole is much cheaper if created out of standardized parts. Indeed, the secret of a whole delivered within a tight budget is to use as many cheap and standardized constituents as is possible. At top left we see that "a dirty great pile of bricks do not make a house." What makes a building or a set of buildings valuable is how the whole has been designed, what it means, what it represents, how aesthetic it is and whether we enjoy occupying it. At bottom right, the designer has been given a totally free hand but the result is likely to be unaffordable. Wholes have to take note of what parts are readily available and how much they cost. Generally speaking, the more standardized the parts, the less costly the whole design will be. Yet roughly assembling the parts in an unplanned way is likely to be neither cheap enough nor of sufficient quality, see middle of illustration. What is needed is a highly original design made out of highly standardized parts and modules. We see this at top right. Once again it is the relationship among values that counts in the end. Has the whole design taken heed of the cost of materials available? Have building blocks that come in the hundreds and thousands been fashioned into a unique design? Recall our definition of creativity as a new relationship among old parts. There is no inherent reason why the parts should not be mass-manufactured in volume to keep costs down. We need a new fusion between simplicity and overall complexity, between cheaper processes and more valuable products, between the parsimony of winter and the luxury of high summer, between the raw and the finished. We are after the reconciliation of contrasting values yet again.

FIVE STAGES IN THE EVOLUTION OF HOW BUSINESS SERVES US

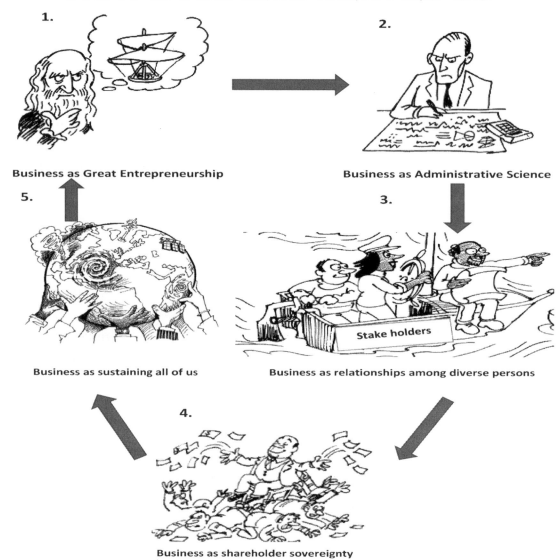

1. Business as Great Entrepreneurship

2. Business as Administrative Science

3. Business as relationships among diverse persons

4. Business as shareholder sovereignty

5. Business as sustaining all of us

SEQUENTIAL PHILOSOPHIES OF BUSINESS

Fons Trompenaars has traced philosophies of Western businesses as going through five stages. In stage 1, the 18th century in Britain and the 19th century in the USA, business was identified with Great Entrepreneurs and inventors, men like Josiah Wedgwood, Andrew Carnegie and Thomas Edison. They personified the companies they had created and mobilized vast resources. But this could not last and, as the twentieth century dawned, they were dying off and the side-kicks on whom their wealth devolved lack legitimacy. What right did they have to wield such power? This crisis ushered in Stage 2, the ideal of Business as an Administrative Science. In 1928 the Harvard Business School was created and business was "mastered" in a class-room. Everything you needed to know could be taught in two years by reading cases! There was "one best way" scientifically proven. Business was a profession. Needless to say, creative genius was missing from the curriculum and handling other's money was emphasised. The accident of the Hawthorne Experiment in the late Thirties gave rise to Stage 3, the Human Relations Movement. Alliances with diverse people, deeply engaged with each other was the secret of success. This rose and peaked in the late 60s and then collided with stage 4. The ideal of Shareholder Sovereignty was promoted by Margaret Thatcher and Ronald Reagan and seen as increasing the level of investment and beating the unions, but instead of promoting faster economic growth, western economies slowed and lost market share to Asia, culminating in the crash of 2008. The latest ideal, stage 5, is about the Sustainability of the entire industrial eco-system and the harmonization of all five elements of the cycle in a circular life-enhancing economy, wherein we become stewards of the environment & take corporate social responsibility for all impacts. Trompenaars shows how these five values constitute ten dilemmas which can be reconciled. All stages are still with us and need fine tuning as social purposes and higher goals.

PART VII

CREATIVITY & INNOVATION:

A RECOURSE FOR DEVELOPED NATIONS

CREATIVITY & INNOVATION: A RECOURSE FOR DEVELOPED NATIONS

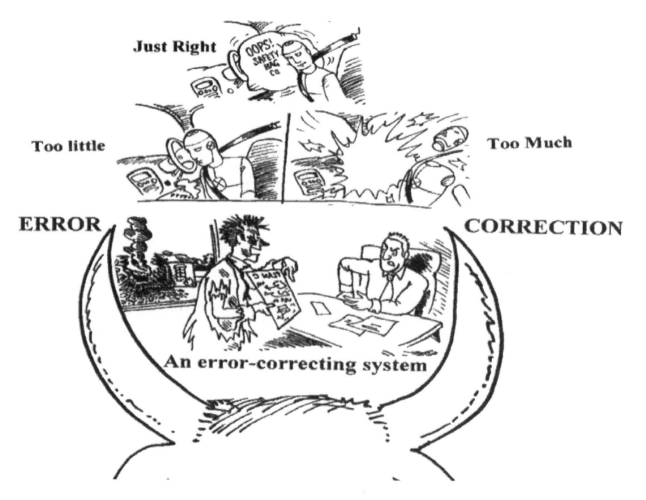

INNOVATION IS AS MUCH PERSPIRATION AS INSPIRATION. GETTING IT JUST RIGHT INVOLVES COUNTLESS TRIALS AND MANY ERRORS.

Creativity works at the level of ideas and new envisioned combinations. Innovation involves translating that new conception into a product/service, bringing it to the market and making enough money to continue operations. Innovation is the concrete realization of creative ideas, enabling these to go forward. Take the example of an airbag that inflates to protect the occupants of an automobile in the event of a collision. Inventing the gas pellet that inflates the bag in a fraction of a second is only the beginning. In order to be commercially successful, the product must be extensively tested. If it expands too little and too slowly it will fail to save the driver. If it expands too far and too fast it could injure or even kill the driver. Getting it just right needs endless trials and experiments with crash-test dummies. There are also major hazards in the manufacture of gas pellets. Individually they are explosive but collectively they could blow your plant sky-high and prove to be a very expensive error! It is therefore essential to have enough process innovation to manufacture the pellets safely.

Almost all new products are full of bugs that have to be eliminated one by one through trial and error and exhaustive efforts at correction of flaws. Not all new ideas appeal to customers. The vast majority of patented ideas are never sold. The notion that all innovation needs is a few geniuses disrupting normal patterns of thought is a non-starter. It takes at least as much perspiration as inspiration. This part will first examine what it takes to create new ideas and then move to what is required to innovate a viable product and/or service that repays all difficulties and re-imposes an orderly system of production. How do you create a corporate culture capable of both creating and developing new products/services? Are we creative exceptions to Nature or should Creation and what she has evolved inspire us? Evolution represents millions of years of improvement in natural designs, as life-forms fit or fail to fit the environment.

∽

A) Acts of creation

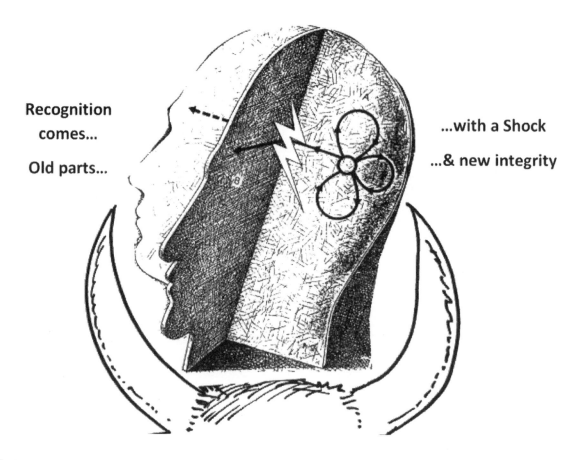

Recognition comes...

Old parts...

...with a Shock

...& new integrity

WE RECOGNIZE SOMETHING CREATIVE BECAUSE THE PARTS ARE NOT NEW, ONLY THEIR COMBINATION. THIS GIVES US A "SHOCK OF RECOGNITION". WE LAUGH IN DELIGHT AT A SATIRIST, ONLY BECAUSE WE RECOGNIZE THE TARGET AND S/ HE IS NOT THAT TARGET BUT IS MIMICKING HIM.

Arthur Koestler's classic *The Act of Creation* explains that new concepts are forged when one thought-matrix suddenly associates with one other or more matrices of thought. He called this "bisociation". The two or three concepts were formerly so far apart from each other that no one had thought of combining them. Take Guttenberg's invention of the printing press. He had watched the operation of a wine-press crushing grapes. He had seen playing cards being made by carving wooden blocks and applying red and black ink to the raised images, then stamped on rectangular pieces of cardboard. He had been to the imperial mint and saw that images impressed on hot metal leave a lasting image on the coin when it cooled. His printing press was an association of these three technologies, heating metal and inscribing it, inking the metal image and pressing it down on paper. In what sense were these three "far apart" from each other? Playing cards, drinking wine and minting money were all very secular, even sinful. What was a man faced with the task of printing Bibles for a pilgrimage to Rome doing in such doubtful company? Note that a printed bible is of far greater significance than wine or playing cards. Combinations may mean more than the sum of their parts. We have used the horns on the bull's head to symbolize the dilemma of the secular and sacred and the very unexpected integration of wine, cards and coins in the printing of a sacred text. Creativity is accompanied by the shock of recognition. We have seen the parts before but all of them being combined is a shock. The combination is new but the parts are old. The lightening stroke is the sudden realization that two worlds are connectable, as was a mild rash suffered by milk-maids (cow-pox) and the ability to immunize everyone against small-pox. Chloroform was a cosmetic for women before it ever served as an anaesthetic. They were even cautioned they might faint!

FIERCE CONCENTRATION AND GENTLE RELAXATION

Mind fiercely focused on the problem

Mind relaxes, wanders, ponders

CREATIVITY IS HELPED BY ALTERNATE FOCUS AND CONCENTRATION ON THE PROBLEM FOLLOWED BY A WANDERING RELAXATION AND PONDERING. YOU HAVE TO BE BOTH IN THE BOX AND OUT OF IT BY TURNS.

We earlier claimed that creativity and innovation had an affinity with dilemmas. Certainly, two very opposed mind-sets are required. Here we look at intense focus on the one hand and letting the mind wander and relax on the other. The story is ancient. Hiero, the tyrant of Syracuse, had been given a silver crown and gave it to his court scientist, Archimedes, to discover whether it was in reality pure silver or had been adulterated by base metals. Archimedes knew the cubic weight of silver and could weigh the crown easily enough but how was he to estimate the volume of so irregular an object? To melt the crown would spoil it. Much of its value was in the filigree ornamentation. The harder he concentrated, the more the solution eluded him. He decided to call it a night and take a bath. As he lowered his body into the bath-tub the water rose, displaced by his body, and the answer occurred to him. He shouted "Eureka! I have found it!" He could immerse the crown in a full bowl of water and measure the volume of water displaced. His body had acted as a metaphor for the answer.

Note that when you relax and stop focusing narrowly on what you are looking for, thoughts wander unbidden into your mind and your sub-conscious gets a chance to ponder. The comedian John Cleese and his team would regularly sleep on how to make their comedy even funnier and sure enough answers would come in the night when they were not trying so hard. Comedy involves the unexpected clash of very different frames producing a Ha-Ha reflex. But just relaxing like some Hippie or drop-out is no answer either. You must know what you are looking for or you will not recognize it when it pops into your mind at an unguarded moment. This focus is every bit as important as the occasional wandering. Creativity comes from switching between the two modes and considering matters that might seem external like a bowl of water, not earlier seen as an element needed for a solution. This helps explain findings by Teresa Amabile at Harvard Business School that putting employees under pressure reduces creativity, as do time-lines and a sense of urgency. These all make relaxing and pondering harder to do. What do you write on your time-sheet?

THE HARE AND THE TORTOISE: POUNCE AND PONDER

THE LEAPING HARE IS THE NEO-CORTEX OF THE BRAIN. IT IS QUICK AND CLEVER. BENEATH LIES THE OLDER BRAIN WHICH PONDERS ON AFFAIRS AND RUMINATES. NEW CONNECTIONS COME FROM THIS RELAXATION.

The human brain has a "thinking cap", the neo-cortex, which is quick, nimble and quite approximate. It is responsible for most of our quick reactions to events, like side-stepping a vehicle bearing down upon us and doing routine tasks. It draws on our ordered habits and makes the appropriate moves to deal with familiar situations. However, there is a deeper brain below the neo-cortex that deals with the new and the unfamiliar. It derives from our older reptilian and mammalian brains and addresses problems to which the neo-cortex cannot see a quick solution. It gets passed down for extended rumination. Guy Claxton, the educational psychologist, has likened this to the Aesop's Fable of the Hare and the Tortoise, in which the two animals race each other. With the hare far ahead and out of sight, he decides to take nap and the tortoise overtakes him. What we need to be innovative and creative is the slowly pondering and ruminating tortoise. It could very well be that we are asking the wrong question and this needs to be reconceived. Einstein famously said that fundamental problems could not be solved at the same level as their initial formulation. We need to re-think the whole issue, which is what happened when Archimedes got into his bath, (see previous page). This act re-formulated the initial task. It brought new elements into the situation. Most interpretations of this story see it as praising perseverance and hard work but Claxton gives it an intriguing twist. The creative mind does not hurry for extraneous reasons like deadlines and demands for speed. It is engaged deeply with a fascinating problem which it turns over in its mind and does not let go. While others sleep, it examines all possibilities and all angles. We saw earlier in Volume 1 that offering money to a team impedes its creative problem solving. The team pounces for the carrot when it should be pondering. We can now see why. American SAT examinations put students under tight deadlines, where speed is regarded as an essential element of ability. When the British author first took such a test they snatched away his paper before he had answered 60% of the questions! Pondering or checking reduces your score. This greatly narrows the definition of ability and may fail more creative persons. It is fine to pounce quickly and smartly on a solution but only if you have pondered first!

DIVERGING THE BETTER TO CONVERGE ON SOLUTIONS

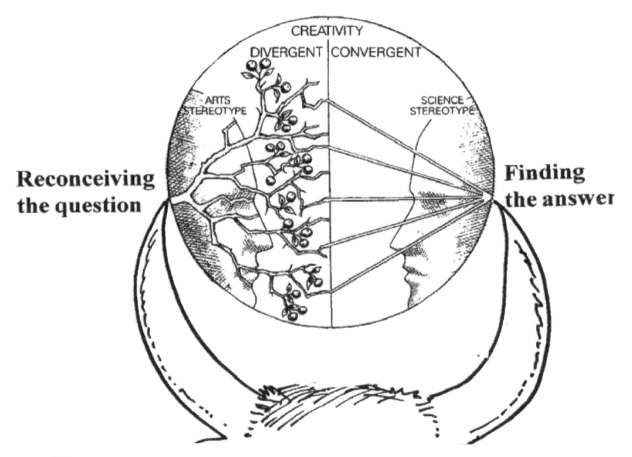

THE MORE YOU HAVE DIVERGED ARTISTICALLY IN YOUR THINKING, THE MORE LIKELY IT IS THAT NEW PERSPECTIVES WILL BE USED IN ANY SCIENTIFIC CONVERGENCE ON A SOLUTION AND THAT THIS WILL BE ORIGINAL.

Research has established that people tend to think divergently and convergently depending on their type of schooling they have had. Arts graduates tend to diverge. They tend to talk more and freely express their opinions. Their views spread out into a wide orbit. Their general knowledge tends to be extensive and they express themselves in colourful language, engaging their listeners rather than proving their points. They use language well and are articulate. They are better at raising issues than at settling them. The person thinking convergently tries to establish facts and choose the right answer which is assumed to exist, and in disciplines like maths, engineering and the hard sciences, it DOES exist. They generally talk less and search out solutions. They are less interested in general knowledge than their own disciplines and tend to solve problems set for them by teachers. They are more exact and talk less to persuade than to inform. They tend to do better in SAT tests and in IQ and they value precision. Creativity requires divergence AND convergence. You must first reformulate the question and redefine it, bringing in elements others have missed and only then, zero in on the answer. The creative scientist resembles the artist in many ways. Having reached the leading edge of her discipline she must invent her own questions and hypotheses and then prove her point by deduction. Opposite, we have likened divergence to the branching out of a tree with blossoms or fruit and convergence to a much more efficient and formalized systems of proof. Divergent people often give the impression of being creative but this is often confined to verbal pyrotechnics. Politicians, for example, give us more words than deeds, more debates and promises than solutions. World-changing technologies are largely the work of engineers and scientists converging and systems being re-drawn. Polarizing, what C.P. Snow called "the two cultures", is an impediment to progress. Genuine innovation lies between these processes.

DIVERGING THEN CONVERGING FORMS A SEARCH PATTERN

Broad divergence & hunt for clues

LATERAL SEARCH

DISCOVERY

VERTICAL THINKING

Converging on a solution

DIVERGENCE IS A SEARCH FOR CLUES IN A WIDE FIELD OF INQUIRY. CONVERGENCE ZEROES IN ON THE MOST PROBABLE ANSWERS.

Whether we are trying to solve a problem, to trace a runaway convict or come up with an innovative solution, diverging must precede converging. Since the escapee may have taken any of many different paths, the bloodhounds first diverge in an attempt to pick up the scent. The broader the area covered, the more likely it is that his scent will be detected. When this occurs, the successful dog howls and the others join him in the chase. The prey is run-down and they converge upon him. The divergent phase involves a lateral search. The convergent phase involves vertical, straight-line pursuit. Note that this applies to many different subjects. In classic psychoanalysis the patient lies on a couch and free-associates about possible symptoms of his neurosis. The psychiatrist is looking for clues and nothing, even sexuality and unconscious processes, are taboo. He will later converge on what he sees as the source of the problem and when this is explained, the patient hopefully recovers. A jury will first hear a wide range of evidence and then reach a verdict. Before pronouncing sentence, a judge will first hear mitigating circumstances and then announce the sentence. A team at work trying to solve a recurring problem will first consider many possibilities. The more of these there are, the more likely it is that two or more insights may combine in a new and creative connection. Midway through the meeting the divergent phase must yield to the convergent phases or no solution will be found by the time the meeting winds up. The early phase is sometimes called a "brainstorm" with all possibilities, however remote, shared around the table. Ideas are thrown on the table in the hope that lateral connections will be found between them and new meanings then pursued vertically to a conclusion. The divergent-convergent distinction was made J W Getzels and P W Jackson in the USA and Liam Hudson in the UK. The contrast between lateral thinking and divergent thinking is by Edward de Bono on the next page.

VERTICAL AND LATERAL THINKING

VERTICAL THINKING SINKS STRAIGHT LINE SHAFTS AND DECLINES TO DIVERGE. IT OFTEN GETS STUCK AND FRUSTRATED. LATERAL THINKING JOINS TWO OR MORE OF THESE SHAFTS AND MAKES NEW CREATIVE CONNECTIONS.

Edward de Bono points out that most of our thinking is vertical and moves in a straight line. This is true of a subject using a verb to impact an object, of stimulus-response, of cause and effect, hypothesis and deduction and of drilling down into the earth for what it can yield, as in the picture opposite. Many of us seek to be rational and this consists of an effect which can be predicted and controlled by us and an end following logically and demonstrably from a means. A syllogism is vertical. "Men die. Socrates is a man therefore Socrates is mortal." However, not all thinking is vertical. Evolution, for example, operates by blind chance, and the collision of entities and whether creatures thrown up against a changing environment will survive is often unknowable. Human relationships are lateral connections and whether they will work or not is a puzzle. Your customers have tastes that can rarely be gauged in advance. But the biggest exception of all to vertical thinking is a lateral connection between vertical shafts illustrated opposite. Take the problem of a surgeon whose patients scream and thrash when he operates on them. He finds his wife passed out on their bed. She opened a jar of chloroform, a cosmetic at that time, and inhaled its fumes by accident. It occurs to the surgeon that it might be to his advantage, and certainly to the advantage of his patients, if they were unconscious when he cut into them. This vital breakthrough is the result of laterally connecting two chains of events. Its importance dwarfs beauty treatments, as well as agonizing surgical operations. Economies and societies advance by dint of their lateral thinking. It is easy to lose sight of this because before creative break-throughs are accepted, they need to be verified and the process of verification is once more vertical. When we put procedures into use they have to be applied, operated and implemented and this too is vertical and rational. It becomes all too easy to believe that lateral thinking hardly counts! Yet without it, economies die, especially advanced economies, because low wage economies can copy our methods cheaply.

Golden Ages: the rare combinations of cash with artistry

Cash from Bankers

Used to honour God through art and science

It is rare for creative and artistic persons to have large infusions of money, but this has historically ushered in Golden Ages.

We have associated creativity with highly improbable combinations of highly diverse elements. One reason Golden Ages are rare and often brief, is that these combinations are infrequent, precarious and may not last. When people find it hard to gain proper nourishment, why would cash be spent on artistic splendours? This does not happen in most countries for most of the time. The amazing comic and tragic plays of Ancient Greece were not entertainment but religion, a courageous examination of the human condition, prone to catastrophic error. The dramas were not only expensive to stage but lavish sums were paid to winning entries with playwrights as local heroes. All this was financed by the owners of silver mines who used slave labour! Perhaps the owners felt a need for spiritual redemption? This was certainly true in the case of the Medici bankers of Florence. Bank loans were condemned as usury by the church and courts were not consistent in supporting repayment. Bankers used gangster methods in order to collect and were surely going to hell. The Medici decided to redeem their souls by sponsoring architecture, painting and science that was to spearhead the Renaissance in Europe. So successful were they that the family rose from predator to papacy and Lorenzo the Magnificent became a patron for classical and biblical arts. Frans Johannson has referred to the "Medici effect", as the unexpected fusion of two or more trends in high tech industry. For example, biology and medicine are likely to produce many antibodies and diagnostic tests. The fusion of mechanical and electrical engineering has already produced a raft of inventiveness called "mechatronics". While it is not possible to predict what will be created, it is possible to predict that fusing disciplines will increase the number of innovations and steer industries towards new syntheses. This is what industrial strategy does.

❦

Playing precedes serious intentions

THE RISK AND THE DANGER IS LARGELY WITHOUT COST

WHERE REALITY IS SIMULATED

Simulation and modelling

Underlying reality

Simulation allows you to play and to pretend and so learn without trauma. It may be a major mark of civilization.

An important source of learning and innovating is the capacity to play. Animals play. Everything a lion or tiger cub needs to learn is rehearsed when playing with other cubs. All that remains is to bare their fangs, extend their claws, get serious and kill. When playing, lips hang over teeth and no harm is done. Human beings put on theatrical plays in which they kill without really killing, weep tears without suffering personal loss and learn all about human greatness and weaknesses. When innovating you experiment playfully, often using simulations. The gift to Cambridge University of CAD equipment (computer aided design) by the Wilson government is often cited as the beginning of the Cambridge Phenomenon. It enabled engineers and scientists to simulate what they were thinking about and detect the flaws which would cost them dear at a later stage.

Modelling, simulating and creating prototypes are all forms of play about which you are ultimately serious, just as tragedy on stage has the serious intention of warning us about human folly before we do anything stupid. When Detroit switched from clay models of new cars to computerized sections it became many times more innovative. The more elaborate and attractive your prototype, the higher quality and the more ingenious will be the final product. Prototypes are heuristic, "serving to find out". Future customers can inspect the prototype and ask for modifications, thus facilitating co-creation. Where the prototype is much cheaper than the finished product, like a virtual reality display of a shopping mall, then this becomes especially valuable. Videos can describe an imagined product in detail, plus its effects on people and on the environment of its use. This could motivate investors to fund such products, and stakeholders to supply and to buy them. Innovation is the key to the economic survival of affluent economies. The fate of nations depends upon it. It is when we play that we ponder, diverge, relax, brainstorm and entertain many possibilities through a sense of fun. Innovation involves many trials and false starts and if these can be done playfully at low cost by people who love what they are doing, then a culture of innovation is engendered. Note also how "inefficient" innovation is. All that messing around, repetition and those foolish errors!

Thinking processes of highly creative architects

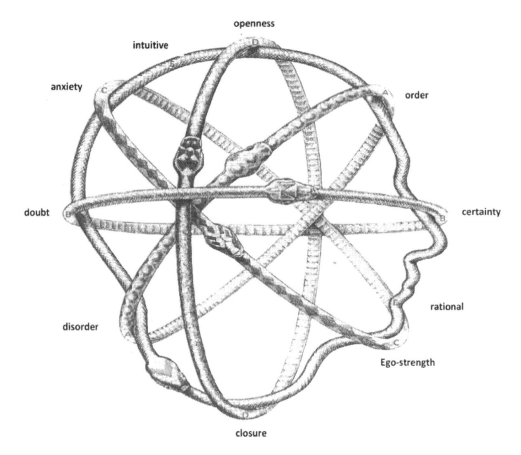

openness

intuitive

anxiety

order

doubt

certainty

rational

disorder

Ego-strength

closure

Creative architects have personality profiles with highly contrasting opposites; doubting and becoming certain, both ordering and disordering, neurotic yet resilient. They are paradoxical.

Frank Barron conducted personality tests on a number of architects designated as highly creative by their peers and contrasted this with a control group of ordinary architects. His creative group were by no means perfect in their conduct as society often defines it. We have used the symbol of Uroboros, the self-devouring snake or dragon of antiquity. It derives from Ancient Egypt and symbolizes the cycle of eternal return, the capacity to re-create oneself, holism, and evolutionary infinity. It was in frequent use during the Renaissance and symbolized the magic of artistry. Here we regard it as a symbol of paradox since who is eating and who is being eaten is ambiguous, as were the values and personalities of these architects. Barron found them surprisingly high in anxiety, often regarded as a symptom of neuroses. They reported being nervous. But they were also very high in ego-strength, i.e. resilience and the power to rally from set-back. He concluded that they took larger risks, worried about the consequences of this, but soon recovered their spirits to risk again. Originality is an existential danger. The meaning of your life is often on the line. You have ventured where others did not dare. Consistent with this are greater doubts but also greater certainty when doubts are removed, more openness followed by greater closure. They used more intuition but checked on this rationally. They disordered their thoughts in the interests of better re-ordering them. Because of these shifts back and forth, they were not always trusted.

B) Innovation requires a critical environment

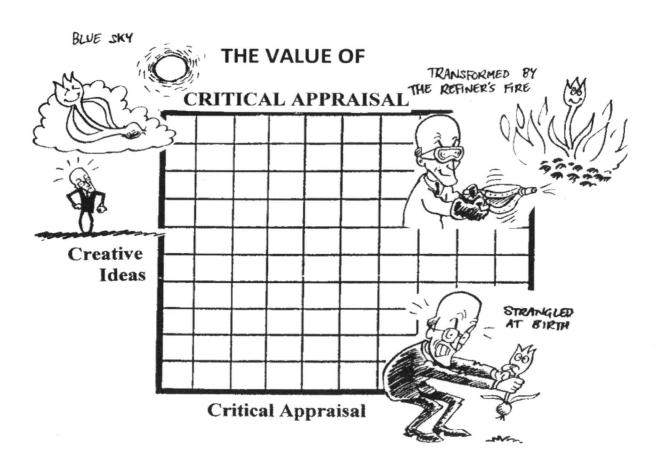

Customers do not buy even the most brilliant idea. It needs to be constructively criticized and turned into a finished product and via a Refiner's Fire, honed to perfection.

Absolutely essential to the quality of saleable innovation is the role of the Critic, what Meredith Belbin has called the Monitor-Evaluator within the team. This is the man with the domed head in the illustration opposite. Such persons are typically highly intelligent and this is witnessed through their analytical and rational powers, which are most in evidence when trashing hare-brained ideas by the Plant (or creative ideas-person). The Plant and the Monitor-Evaluator tend to rile one another. The Plant loves playing with ideas at top left but if s/he spells out exactly what this means, the Monitor Evaluator will be all over her/him with cutting objections. The temptation is to engage in "blue sky" theorizing and not come down to earth with an actionable project. The ME is pictured waiting impatiently. When the Plant does eventually come down to earth the angry Critic sets about him and the idea is often "strangled at birth", after all, enough time has been wasted already! What is needed is constructive criticism. Customers do not buy even the most brilliant idea. They buy finished products of those ideas with all their bugs eliminated. Even the best idea needs a considerably amount of work to raise its appeal and ready it for the market. Originality is not enough. It must meet existing needs. We have used the metaphor of the Refiner's Fire at top right. The refiner can purify a precious metal by heating it and extracting any impurities. All new products can be improved and made even more valuable. But note that the Critic must be accepting of the Plant's originality, must be on her/his side, must want the project to succeed. The display of his critical powers is not sufficient. Belbin once formed a team consisting entirely of super-intelligent critics and had them compete against teams with lesser talents. The Monitor-Evaluators came last! They had all demolished each other.

ॐ

INNOVATION NEEDS DIFFERENCES TO BE INTEGRATED

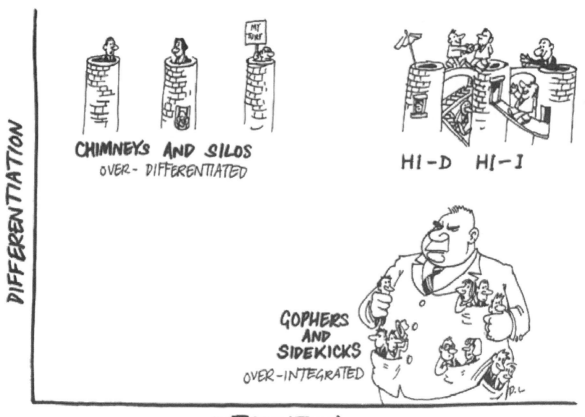

THE MOST INNOVATIVELY SUCCESSFUL PLASTICS COMPANIES WERE FOUND TO BE **BOTH** HIGHLY DIFFERENTIATED **AND** HIGHLY INTEGRATED. THE MODEL WAS FROM BIOLOGY NOT PHYSICS.

Creativity cannot be converted into innovation unless the new ways of operating essential to innovation are integrated into the organization. Adam Smith wrote much about the division of labour. He saw this as the foundation stone of creating wealth. He put less emphasis on the integration of labour because the businesses of his time were mostly small and a single leader could easily connect employees with one another. However, where the number of employees grow beyond 150 or so, formal procedures for working together get introduced and how well diverse activities get integrated becomes a vital consideration. Paul Lawrence and Jay Lorsch at Harvard measured the extent to which companies were differentiated into separate functions and the extent they were integrated by leaders, or in many cases by project groups, in the style of NASA which has teams which create the modules needed for space flight and vehicle assembly. Top left we see a company so badly over-differentiated that its functions will resemble "chimneys" or "grain silos". Such organizations kill creative ideas because they are already unable to reach each other and anything new would make things worse. The same applied to organizations that are over integrated and the leader tries to hold people together, see bottom right. Under these circumstances anything new challenges his hold on people and inventors challenge his authority. The authors compared the then highly innovative plastics industry with routine cardboard box suppliers. In plastics, successful innovation required both high differentiation AND high integration for the company to be successful. To make cardboard boxes this was not needed. Differentiation by itself is not enough to make you innovative, nor is integration by itself. Both are needed in combination. Only these kinds of organizations can play host to innovative activities.

∽

c) Erring, correcting and continuously improving I

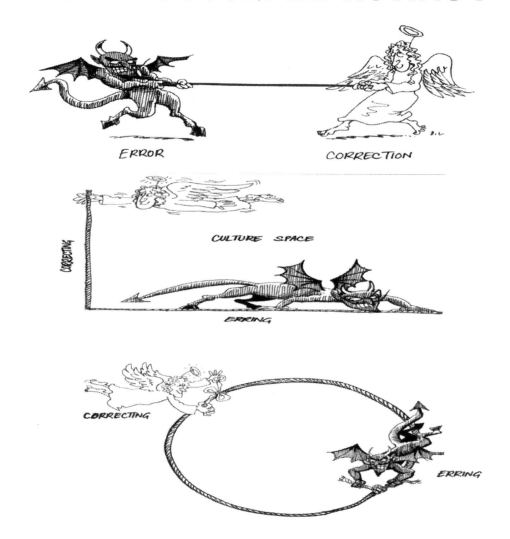

From a line, to a dual axis, to a loop.

Here we take a fresh look at good and evil. It begins with an eternal tug of war between the two. (picture at top). We must crush evil! Alas, this crushing is often an evil in itself! Indeed, one must be more evil in order to crush the enemy if by this is meant more destruction; the victor is usually the best killer, witness the body count in Vietnam while the President was praying. But, once we are willing to admit mistakes or have this verdict indict us, then this is transformed into error and correction and we can create a culture space in which accidental or negligent errors can be examined and put right (middle picture). Note that these errors must be unintentional, not deliberately compounded. Error is also self- defined so the higher we aspire, the more errors there will be and the more must these be tolerated where people are doing their best. We get what we want by successive approximations to an ideal being sought after. If 30% of what we do is "wrong", we are for ever striving to improve and raise our standards. It is but a small step from here to create a learning loop for the systematic correction of errors leading to continuous improvement and ever greater aspirations, (see next page).

৯৬

Erring, correcting and continuously improving II

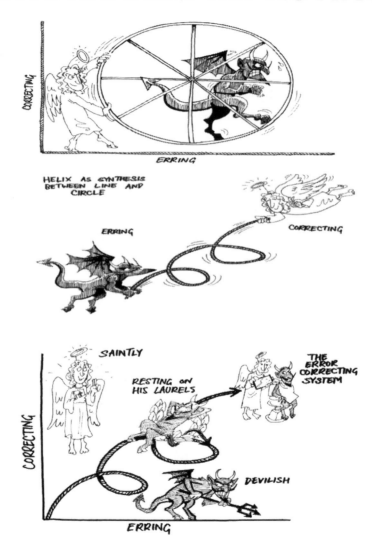

Setting up the error-correcting system.

At the top errors are being corrected, but in a punitive way. One problem with this is that errors will not be admitted, people will hide them away and blame someone else, so we cannot learn from them, or they are attributed to human sinfulness, when a better system could have helped eliminate them. In the middle we create a helix which gives our learning loop a sense of direction, e.g. higher quality production by eliminating bugs. This is a synthesis of a line and a circle and includes both values, while having a forward direction to ever greater excellence. Note again that failure is relative to the standards you are aiming to achieve. You MUST make "errors" if you aim to do better over time. You do not know what is possible until you have tried. At bottom we 'give the devil a haircut' and we must not let him rest on his laurels, but rather push on. Fallible people are operating an error correcting system and continuously learning while improving. You learn more from negative than from positive feedback. The former is more arresting and surprising. Note that without the news that you can do better, no improvement will take place. The higher we aspire, the more mistakes we make. If errors are only 0.5%, we may fall asleep and the work-place would cease to be challenging! The battle with "error" must never cease and we must always ask more of ourselves. Some "errors" we make may turn out to be better than we intended, in which case we can use even accidents to improve our methods and processes. We need to distinguish process innovation from product innovation. Much of East Asia excels at the former. They note what we want to buy and produce it much more innovatively than we do. We accuse them of copying us but the processes of manufacture are often highly original and relationships with the work-force much better.

D) INNOVATION MUST BE OPEN TO THE LARGER ECO-SYSTEM

CLOSED INNOVATION

OPEN INNOVATION

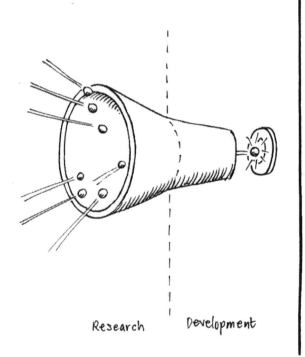

Research   Development

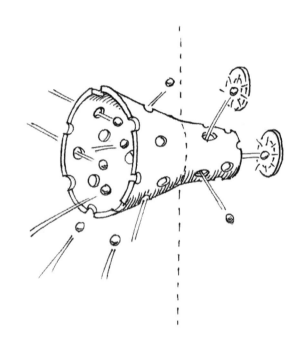

YOUR INNOVATIVE STRATEGIES AND PURPOSES MUST BE OPEN TO THE ENTIRE ECO-SYSTEM SURROUNDING THE COMPANY IF YOU ARE TO ENLIST ITS ASSISTANCE AND ITS INGENUITY. CREATIVITY REQUIRES NEW ELEMENTS TO COMBINE IN NEW WAYS.

In the left-hand picture innovation occurs within a single company and stems usually from the R&D department. It is kept secret in order to surprise rivals. Everyone else, even suppliers, customers, sub-contractors partners, and your own employees are not told and kept in the dark. The problem with this is that you may require help from several stakeholders to be a genuinely innovative system. "The world's safest car" will need input from those who supply braking-systems, reinforced steel, seat-belts, air-bags, automatically unlocking doors, anti-skid devices and the capacity to take back control from an ailing driver. Solar panels for roofs will need any recent breakthrough in photovoltaic cells. Customers and dealers will need to be alerted in advance in order to be ready. In effect, the whole industrial ecosystem must be allowed to penetrate the boundaries of the company and innovate as a single alliance of stakeholders. The system must be open to new devices from suppliers which are needed. Most innovation in the automobile industry is electronic, supplied from the outside. It does not follow that you are in the auto-business. Why not be in the Global Positioning Market and sell to other auto-makers? Why not be in the car-loans business? Why not provide businesses with a "mobile office?"

Is innovation internal to a company or external?

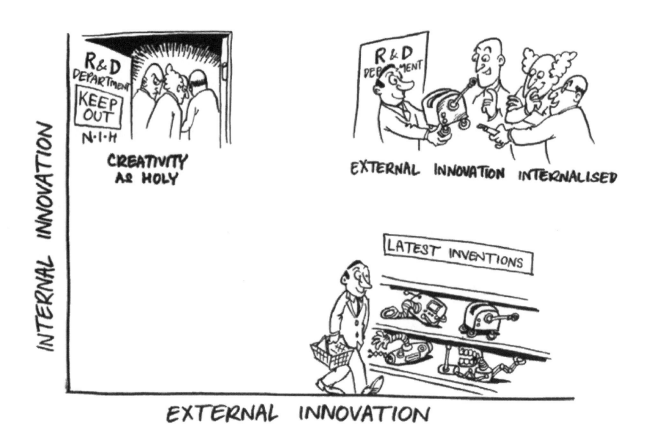

THERE ARE TWO SOURCES OF INNOVATION FOR ANY COMPANY - THOSE LYING INSIDE THE COMPANY AND THOSE LYING OUTSIDE IT.

The commonest attitude to innovation is that it is inside the company and within certain people within that company. It is most commonly associated with Research and Development. The more a company spends on this, the more innovative it will supposedly be. There are several comparisons between nations on how much they spend on R&D; Germany, South Korea and Sweden tend to be high, but this is far from a guarantee that they will be more innovative. One reason is that R&D is but one form of innovation, the kind generated internally, usually by large companies. Too often this is kept secret and exclusive within the company, a holy font of genius, suffering from the NIH syndrome, (Not Invented Here) and hence inferior. Work done on the outside tends to be underestimated. In the days when IBM could afford to employ 80% of America's leading computer scientists, this made some sense but this situation has long gone. Big corporations have difficulty with being innovative in any case. The vast majority of new ventures come from small, start-up companies. Silicon Valley was an example of this. Xerox Parc spent lavishly on R&D but it was people quitting this effort who prevailed as individual entrepreneurs, once they were free of Xerox. This means that more and more innovation comes from projects outside R&D departments and that large companies can buy these up and add them to their portfolios. But this is full of peril too. When you pay a young entrepreneur tens of millions for a small company, s/he will take the money and start over again. What you have acquired is missing the very spirit that made it great. You have a temporary income stream but the inspiration has flown. Big companies have too much to lose to take many risks and their existing businesses shape how they think and conceive, crushing new ways of thinking. It is not enough to have directors of internal and external innovation as does Proctor and Gamble, the two streams of knowledge must learn from one another and move in the directions where breakthroughs are most likely, see top right of picture.

E) Cambridge Phenomenon:
Economy of the Future?

KNOWLEDGE HAS A TREE-LIKE STRUCTURE WITH ITS ROOTS IN FAMOUS UNIVERSITIES LIKE STANFORD AND CAMBRIDGE. TECHNOLOGY CONSULTANTS CAN MAKE A BIG DIFFERENCE BY EXPLAINING THE COMMERCIAL APPLICATIONS OF RECENT SCIENTIFIC DISCOVERIES.

Governments sponsor education and higher learning holds the key to economic success. Oxford and Cambridge are both 800 years old. Britain's industrial revolution passed by both universities with barely the wave of a hand. Their ethos was monastic, "a haven from the purely practical", an "adorable dreamer" as Matthew Arnold put it. Higher learning was not to be sullied by commerce. The life of the mind needed tranquil surroundings as far from industry as possible. As recently as the mid-seventies, Cambridge had a jam factory, a radio factory, plans for an airfield and that was it, perhaps $400 million. Today, the Cambridge Phenomenon is worth at least $80 billion. Rooted firmly in the knowledge of the university, it looks increasingly like foreshadowing the economy of the future. We have chosen the weeping willow tree as its symbol. The first sign that things might change came from the founding of Cambridge Consultants. Funded by the Ministry of Supply (now the Ministry of Defence), its mission was to describe the science of the university in terms that industry might understand. Its reports were eagerly read but very few actually acted on the recommendations and ventured. Frustrated at having their advice ignored, the staff began to sally forth themselves. Other consultants joined them, and formed companies such as PA, Sagentia and The Technology Partnership. The translation of science into commercial opportunities expanded. From each branch of science and technology off-shoots developed. Several ventures failed, such as Acorn, the first PC, but technologies behind them continued to grow, offering opportunity after opportunity in the market place. These came generation after generation as one product gave birth to the next. Young entrepreneurs working for their ex-professors would spin out on their own with his/her blessing, co-investment and scientific advice and all would remain as part of the growing knowledge tree.

Innovation and the University's diversity of knowledge

What connects the Swedish nocturnal moth to a new resin for making discs?

Universities are probably among the most diverse thinking places in the world. Little wonder that Silicon Valley grew up around Stanford, Rte. 128 around Harvard & MIT, that Harvard is building its Allston Campus around problem-centred and opportunity-centred interdisciplinary studies and, that the Cambridge Phenomenon has grown prodigiously around that university. The illustration opposite pictures the late Gordon Edge consulting colleagues on how evolution has stopped moonlight being reflected from the eye of the Swedish nocturnal moth, so that predators cannot see any gleam. He got together scholars from biology, zoology, physics, mathematics, and material science. He learned that the moth's eyes absorb the entire colour spectrum. It was thought that a plastic could be designed and manufactured for compact discs which would also absorb the entire colour spectrum. The eye was modelled, hugely amplified by Bob Pettigrew using an intraperometer and its properties carefully studied. The result was a polycarbonate that absorbed every wavelength of light and is now in use in millions of CDs that record colour. A large number of innovative products cut across disciplines. Nature does not respect how we have bureaucratized ourselves. This explains why so many new products come from the vicinity of universities rather than the university itself. Departments have produced innovative products but nearby start-ups have produced many more. Departments are still after Nobel Prizes awarded for their purity of discipline, while start-ups can find talent from all over the university and make rare combinations. This process is facilitated by the medieval genius of the college system that also introduces disciplines to each other in cloisters across the dinner table and in common rooms.

The Spin-off and the Parent Offspring Relationship

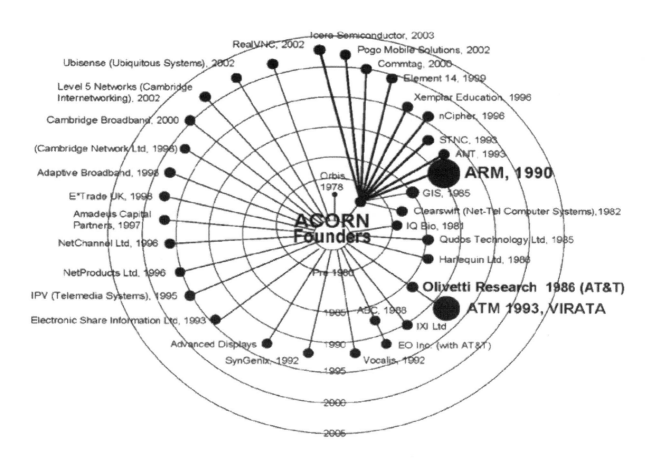

A spin-out, as compared to a spin-off, retains the knowledge and caring bond between parent and offspring, a network of mostly small companies, related by shared science results.

Elizabeth Garnsey at the Institute for Manufacturing at Cambridge University, has mapped a local phenomenon called the spin-out. We have long known that innovative industries cluster in particular regions. If you want to take advantage of the knowledge generated by the university then you locate nearby in order to recruit qualified people and be proximate to rivals and learn what they are doing. Clustering also attracts suppliers and sub-contractors with specialized skills who serve that community. But the spin-out should not be confused with the spin-off. When a group of employees spin-off, they take a project they have been working on away from the company that paid them to work on it and strike out on their own. The ethics of this is at least questionable. The spin-out anticipates that younger people in your organization way wish to start their own companies and offers to invest in these ventures and share scientific knowledge as it emerges from the university. It is similar to family relationships with parents whose children leave home but still keep in close touch.

What the chart opposite illustrates is the technological success of what happened to be a commercial failure. Acorn Computers and Apple 1 were the world's two first PCs. Apple had the larger market, in part because the California government bought one for every high school in the state. However, several of the features of the Acorn found a place in other technologies and start-ups, most especially ARM, a $12 billion chip design company. The chart opposite shows the family of companies spawned by Acorn, the world's most successful "failure". Note that these companies are joined by sciences and "branches" and "twigs" of sciences. No one is in a better position to invest wisely than someone who taught that student personally and witnessed the work being done. It all ends in a knowledge network fed by university research.

❧

f) The We Company: Designing a Culture of Innovation

FORMERLY KNOWN AS WEWORK, THE COMPANY SELLS OFFICE SPACES THAT ENCOURAGE INTERACTION AMONG THE CREATIVE AND THE INNOVATIVE. CAN OFFICE DESIGN DO THIS?

Critics of the We Company refer to it as a real estate company with an aura of pure hype, yet this cannot explain why a company renting out work spaces, has 10 million square feet of office space, 283 offices in 75 world cities, a quarter of a million members and is estimated to be worth $50 billion, all generated since 2010. It has attracted investment from Goldman Sachs, Softbank and JP Morgan. So why do so many young people with dreams of innovation flock to it? It has designed a culture of innovation. We have applied dilemma theory to what the company says. This book is full of dilemmas to which We Company offers solutions. It makes small companies more equal to large ones, by giving them space, health insurance and shared amenities that can be booked. The free beer, coffee, kitchen and dining spaces have a design to bring highly individualistic people together into a community. The two founders, Adam Neumann and Miguel McKelvey, were raised in an Israeli kibbutz and Oregon commune respectively and aim for "kibbutz capitalism". We have seen in this section that creativity requires energetic focus followed by relaxation, just what this environment provides. It encourages face-to-face authentic interaction in a society plagued by internet venom and scams, thereby providing freedom WITH responsibility. In a society given over to consumption and seeing production as a wearisome prelude, it brings joy and self-fulfilment back to work and urges members "to make a life not a living." It is flipping hamburgers that will be automated, not changing the world through innovation. Citibank has taken offices there, so loans are a few yards away, fusing money with artistry. We have seen that innovation needs diversity fused with inclusion. Rarely have so many diverse dreamers congregated in one place. Work-life balance is achieved when work most resembles home and play becomes serious. Innovation requires that we diverge to later converge. It is hard to conceive of an environment friendlier to divergence; new sights and sounds crowd in around you. "Do what you love" says the flag illustrated opposite. The organization has provided a whole culture for otherwise small parts of an answer. It seeks to "elevate the world's consciousness", no less.

PART VIII

WHAT CAN WE DO TO REMEDY THIS CRISIS?

Sustain what sustains us

To see the World in a grain of sand
And Heaven in a wild flower
To hold Infinity in the palm of your hand
And Eternity in an hour

William Blake

IF WE BLESS THE EARTH IT WILL BLESS US AND PROVIDE FOR US. THE HUMAN SPECIES MUST PRESERVE ALL SPECIES AND EXTINCTION MUST STOP. THIS WILL REQUIRE THE SHARED EFFORTS OF ALL STAKEHOLDERS WORKING WITH, AND HARNESSING THE EARTH'S NATURAL FORCES.

Instead of arguing whether our world is in the peril that many think it is, and we generally endorse this sense of urgency, we should dwell on the obvious advantage of working with the earth's natural forces instead of against them. If we can somehow join people, planet and prosperity, then we will be far better off while leaving a healthy planet for our children's children. The evidence is that helping to sustain the earth is more exciting and motivating than just making objects. Employees given this challenge will take it up with gusto. A super-ordinate goal represents a higher purpose and gives meaning to our lives. Interface Carpets announced it would have zero emissions from its many plants by 2020 and is well on its way while making better profits than ever before and winning the admiration of the industry and even Wall Street. Michael Porter has argued that only the private sector has the ability to scale up its efforts to a sufficient size to change capitalism. Small NGOs and brains alone can never do it on their own and are competing for funds with their begging bowls out. They lack the momentum. It is the shared strategies of large corporations, bringing their stakeholders with them, which have the scale to solve global problems. How we relate to the earth which is our habitat is crucial. Evolution is about fitting in to our environment and sustaining it while it sustains us. Sunlight, wind and tide are eternal forces that cost us nothing save the technologies of capture and storage which grow more efficient over time. We look to a future where energy costs ever less, where if we bless the earth, it will bless us, where the human animal preserves all species, where extinction stops.

A) WORK WITH THE EARTH'S NATURAL FORCES
THE TRIPLE BOTTOM LINE

Triple bottom line: People, Planet and Prosperity

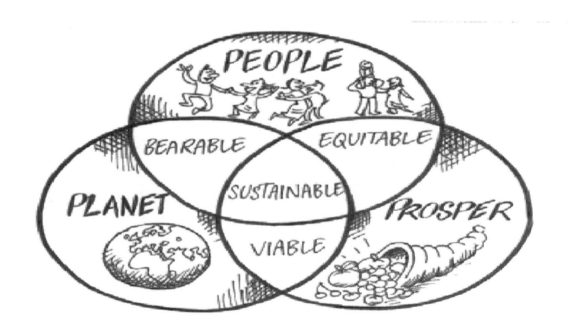

"IT IS LACK OF HUMAN CONSCIOUSNESS THAT HAS RENDERED MOTHER EARTH, THE VERY BASIS OF OUR EXISTENCE, INTO A COMMODITY WITH AN EXPIRY DATE... WE MUST ACT NOW." SADHGURU

The Triple Bottom Line (TBL) was a phrase coined by John B Elkington in his book *Cannibals with Forks*. This can be traced back to an article by Freer Speckley on social audits, but it was Elkington who gave it wide currency. It was very speedily adopted by the Royal Dutch Shell in its sustainability report of 1994, so the idea has put down deep roots in the Netherlands and has been adopted by the 50 or so banks which are members of the Global Alliance of Banking in Values, the co-founder of which, Triodus, is also Dutch. People, Planet and Prosperity (sometimes rendered as Profit) are a series of overlapping spheres, capable of being pushed together to create more shared space. They not only co-exist, they synergise, so that people share in improving the planet and generating prosperity. The Planet and its natural forces like sunshine and wind help us to Prosper, and Prosperity including all People, not the few rich, serve as stewards of the Planet. The place where all three circles overlap spells out SUSTAINABILITY and the larger this area the better. In addition, we can only Prosper if the relationship between money and our Planet is VIABLE. The Planet can only accommodate so many people so that this relationship must be BEARABLE. Finally, the relationship between People and Prosperity must be EQUITABLE. TBL assumes a stakeholder form of capitalism, not just shareholders concerned with their own Prosperity and that the meaning of work involves all three objectives. It is endorsed by B (Benefit) Corporations and by the Conscious Capitalism movement. Audit companies like KPMG are trying to assess the true value of infrastructure projects and their impact on the environment.

Ascending Mount Sustainability

Tomorrow's Child, my daughter-son
I'm afraid I've just begun
To think of you and of your good,
Though always having known I should.

Begin I will to weigh the cost
Of what I squander; what is lost
If ever I forget that you
will someday come to live here too.

Glen Thomas (Employee) read at
Ray Anderson's memorial service

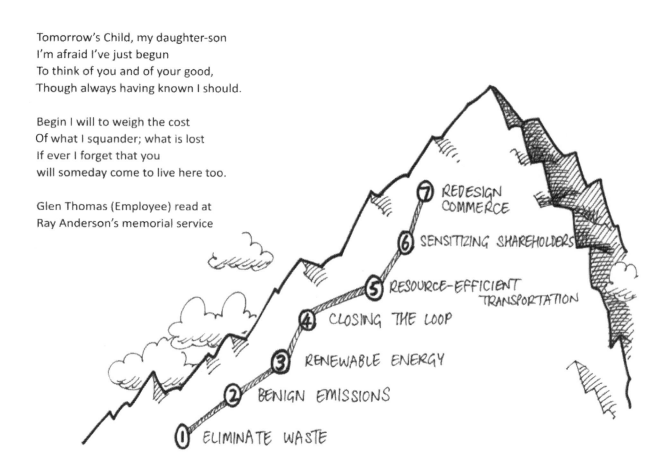

⑦ REDESIGN COMMERCE
⑥ SENSITIZING SHAREHOLDERS
⑤ RESOURCE-EFFICIENT TRANSPORTATION
④ CLOSING THE LOOP
③ RENEWABLE ENERGY
② BENIGN EMISSIONS
① ELIMINATE WASTE

The Seven steps to the summit of the mountain

Ray Anderson, an engineer from Georgia Tech. was founder and CEO of Interface Carpets and was winding up a moderately successful career when, in 1993, he was asked to speak on the subject of the environment. He consulted a book by Paul Hawken and Amory and Hunter Lovins, entitled *Natural Capitalism*. It stunned him. Carpets are 90% oil, from their nylon tufts to their acrylic backing. They are disposed of in landfill. He suddenly saw himself as plundering and polluting the earth and thought to himself, "My God someday they'll send people like me to jail!" He pledged himself to zero emissions by 2020 but died in 2010 when more than half-way to his goal. He detailed his efforts in *Business Lessons from a Radical Industrialist*. We have illustrated what he did opposite. Step 1 was to eliminate waste, described by Anderson as "profits left on the factory floor." He instituted QUEST, which gave employees a share of the savings they had identified and eliminated. The programme was very enjoyable and by 2008 had saved $260 million and the company was numbered among "the Best Companies to work for" by Fortune. Step 2 was to assure that emissions from plants were benign. QUEST was central to this too but it also involved getting suppliers to rid what they supplied of toxins. Their numbers were halved so that those left had such large contracts and incentives, that they would oblige their Interface Carpet customer. Several plants were run on methane gas. This not only eliminates the gas by burning it but makes more room in landfill sites. Step 3 was to convert to Renewable energy wherever possible. At first the cost looked prohibitive but Cool Carpets won a massive contract from the University of California which more than paid for it. Step 4 was to "close the loop" by recycling. He managed to reclaim 200 million tons of carpet, by dint of leasing it not selling it. That way the company still owned the carpet and got it back. He also purchased a separator machine that stripped nylon from acrylic. Step 5 was to revolutionize transportation costs using canals, rivers and seas and use Subaru trucks which have lowest emissions and use the EPA's smart-way calculator to cut costs. Trees were planted for all plane journeys. Step 6 was to work on shareholders and convince them that they were better off as a result of these efforts. The final step was to help redesign commerce, see the next page.

～ક્ર～

PROFITING FROM SAVING THE ENVIRONMENT

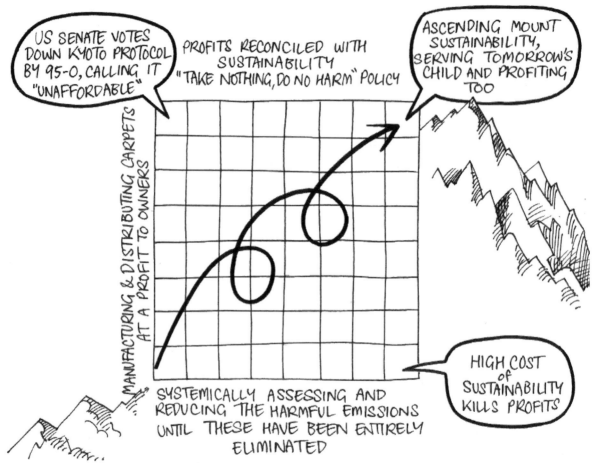

ANDERSON TOOK THE GOALS OF THE KYOTO PROTOCOL, MULTIPLIED THEM BY FIVE AND ACHIEVED THEM WHILE DOUBLING PROFITS AND MARKET SHARES, A "HERO OF THE ENVIRONMENT".

I s it possible for Ray Anderson and Interface Carpets (see previous page) to make profits in the process of saving the environment? Is it possible to succeed in such efforts and win renown in one's society? On the vertical axis opposite, the US Senate, under George W Bush, voted down the very modest, voluntary goals of the Kyoto protocol by 95-0. They were pronounced unaffordable. Ray Anderson took these goals, multiplied them by five, and greatly increased market share and his profits while he chased them. Nor did he want for applause. *Time* magazine hailed him as "Hero of the Environment". Barak Obama appointed him to the Chair of his Council for Sustainable Development. He was written up in the *New York Times, Fortune* and *Fast Company*. In one sense he had always been ahead of the game. His company made carpet tiles. Carpets rarely wear-out evenly. Near the door or under chairs at tables they wear out quickly. Under the table or in unfrequented corners they last indefinitely. By replacing tiles, carpets last four times longer. Anderson's record speaks for itself. By the year before his death (2009) he had reduced carpets sent to landfill by 80%, reduced fresh water use by 80%, and total use of energy was down 43%, with fossil fuel use down by 60%. He had reduced greenhouse gas emissions (with offsets) by 94%. 30% of all the energy he used was renewable, plus 89% of all electricity. 36% of all raw materials were either re-cycled or nourished the earth. 106,000 trees had been planted to offset flights. Waste reduction had netted $433 million. All this was done while increasing profits and market share. Wall Street gave him the cold shoulder until his financial results came through, which piqued their interest. His conclusion was that the whole make-take-waste system had to be redesigned. He believed that new technology can reduce not create waste, by separation, recycling, de-toxifying, and using wind, sun and tides for energy. We need a spiritual and cultural transformation. Making carpets is OK but saving the environment speaks of higher purpose. To achieve this, all stakeholders need to cooperate and work as one.

CRADLE TO CRADLE: PRODUCTS WHICH REGENERATE

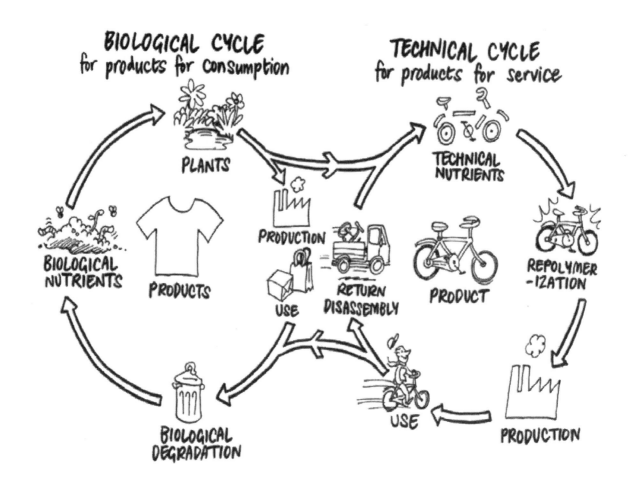

**PRODUCTS CAN BE "BORN AGAIN"
AND HAVE TWO OR MORE LIVES**

We assume that products, like people, are born, grow to maturity and then die. But this is not necessarily so, say William McDonough, an American architect and Michael Braungart, a German chemist, the co-authors of *Cradle to Cradle*. Products can, with the right design, be "born again" and go from cradle to a new cradle. But this can only occur if we make an effective separation between biological and technical ingredients and re-cycle these separately even where these are fused in the production process. Opposite are illustrated the Biological and Technical cycles of a circular economy. Biological ingredients can degrade into valuable nutrients. Take the example of a tree that wastes nothing. The falling leaves enrich the soil. The nuts or kernels of fruit may, with the aid of squirrels start another tree. The aim of the authors is to eliminate the whole notion of waste. These are transformations into something new. Some animal slurry can be converted into high-grade nitrate fertilizer. This is known as up-cycling. Sometimes the residue of a product no longer usable as intended is less valuable than it once was. This is down-cycling. However, it is still more valuable than waste. With clever design, a product can have two or even more lives. Much of what is called "waste" comes from mixing the biological with the technical components and not being able to separate these. Hence if you crush a car with wool and cotton upholstery you get very impure steel with limited strength or uses. If the car is designed to be easily stripped down the separate ingredients are more valuable and the steel can go into new cars and the cotton into new products with considerable savings. Modern vehicles can be disassembled in minutes. Products are part of an eco-system that evolves. The more usefully they can fit with a myriad of other components, the more valuable they become. All this can be influenced by product design. What happens to a product that no longer serves its original purpose? How many other purposes might it then serve? Can it be designed to have life after life? As in so many other ways, creation is our guide to creativity. Evolution has had millions of years to create marvels even before we came into the picture. We should learn from it.

❧

THE GREENING OF OUR CITIES MEANS...

GARDEN ROOFS STABILIZE TEMPERATURES,
PREVENT FLOODING, COOL THE AIR ABOVE CITIES,
PROVIDE RECREATION AND GENERATE OXYGEN.

According to William McDonough and Michael Braungart, a roof with a garden on top of it will last longer than a roof with no garden. The building will be cooler in summer and warmer in winter and has been found to save energy to the tune of $37,000 a year for a single building in Toronto. Indeed, this is the first city in the Western hemisphere to mandate a roof garden on all new construction. Its example has been followed by Copenhagen and Stuttgart. If you fly into Stuttgart airport you will see more greenery on roofs than on the ground! The roof can grow flowers and/or local vegetables. It can be used for recreation, for dining, drinking and dancing. It can have solar and wind energy turbines so that the building is energy-self-sufficient, a practice widely followed by IKEA which uses the flat roofs of its many stores. London boasts a Sky Roof Garden and a John Lewis roof garden, tended by the Garden Society. Baton Rouge in the USA has 128 roof gardens. There is one of many on City Hall in Chicago. In 2009, Chicago added 600,000 square feet of garden and the pace has accelerated since. Washington DC added 190,000 in the same year. There is one on the roof of the US postal service in midtown Manhattan which is 2.5 acres wide. Brooklyn is known for its roof-top farms. San Francisco's Kaiser Rooftop Garden is a major tourist attraction, as is the one atop the Oakland Museum. Green city gardens absorb the nitrogen in the atmosphere and turn it into life-sustaining oxygen. They combat carbon monoxide from car exhausts in the streets below. They soak up heavy rains and release the water gradually while flooded storm-drains cause floods and havoc and often get into the sewage system with ruinous results.

HARNESSING THE SUN AND WIND TO REACH THE TIPPING POINT

THE COST OF ENERGY COULD FALL IN PERPETUITY. WE NEED ONLY PAY FOR CAPTURE AND STORAGE, THE TECHNOLOGIES OF WHICH WILL IMPROVE OVER TIME.

What is the tipping point illustrated opposite? It is the time and the place when Renewable Energies and Fossil Fuel Energies, (coal, gas and oil), achieve price parity. At the moment, the cost of solar and wind is falling fast. Between 4 and 7 years hence, price parity will be achieved and when that happens the few of us who care about the environment will be joined by the billions who want their energy to be cheaper. Why are we so sure of this? Because the natural forces of sun, wind, tide and temperature are inexhaustible. They will last and last. They are a source of energy which is free, while we must drill deeper for oil and coal, kill each other to get access, clean up afterwards and deplete stocks. As of now, renewables are hard going, see the gritted teeth of those climbing to the summit. Renewables cost more and customers dislike the surcharge they must pay. Fierce efforts must be made to climb. But once the tipping point is reached the cost of energy will fall in perpetuity. This is because all we have to pay for is not the energy itself, but the costs of capturing and storing it. As technology improves over time this will cost less and less; the sun beams down upon 173,000 terawatts of energy per day, of which we use 15! Instead of contrived arguments about whether or not the globe is warming - money paid to deniers will never cease - we must wake up to the glaringly obvious truth that it is much cheaper and more effective to work with natural forces than against them. The reason for environmentalism is that we can harness its many benefits and sail with wind and tide behind us. At the moment, China has 75% of the world's solar technology and it is clearly bent on getting to the tipping point first. In eleven Chinese provinces, renewable energy is already cheaper than fossil fuels. When will we wake up? The real Apollo was God of the sun. The moon is dead. There is no market there, which may explain US and UK government policies. Markets must be ceded to private enterprise! In the meantime, we are cutting subsidies within sight of the winning post. Are we mad?

❧

Industrial symbiosis: relating waste to raw materials

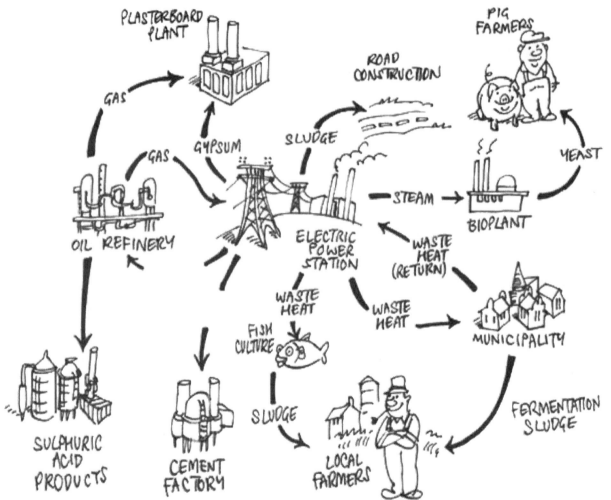

Businesses and farms can cluster in a way that makes use of one another's by-products and "waste" as a single network or eco-system.

Time was when wealth was created by individual proprietors. Then came the age of the corporation, but this too is beginning to fade, despite some corporations being larger and richer than nations. This is because more effective than even big companies, is the entire industrial ecosphere surrounding major operators. If these can prove effective, wealth will be generated in abundance. It takes more than just an automobile company to create the world's safest car; what about those supplying air-bags, anti-lock brakes, seat-belts, thumb-print recognition, crumple-zones around the driver, high-tensile steel etc? In short, you need suppliers, customers, insurers and many other stakeholders. A variation on this is industrial symbiosis, where one company uses the waste products or by-products of another company as raw material or as components. Municipalities receive and return such energy. The illustration opposite is from the Danish town of Kalundborg which has the most advanced example of industrial ecology in the world, with Novo Nordisk, Statoil and Novozymes among the best-known companies participating. It exemplifies public private partnerships as well as industry, agriculture and township. Among the resources exchanged are steam, ash, gas, heat, sludge, and water. It saves 3 million cubic metres of fresh water a year and constitutes a closed circle. 150,000 tons of yeast has replaced 70% of the soy protein formerly needed to feed pigs. Steve Evans of the Institute for Manufacturing at Cambridge University pointed out that carbon dioxide as waste from British Sugar is piped to nearby tomato growers, (the vegetable loves the gas) along with betaine sold to pharmacies, irradiated top-soil and stones sold to garden centres, greens sold to feed pigs plus electricity sold back to the Grid. Nothing is wasted at all and profits are only exceeded by its own operations in China.

෴

B) New alliances: 1. NGOs and for-profit companies

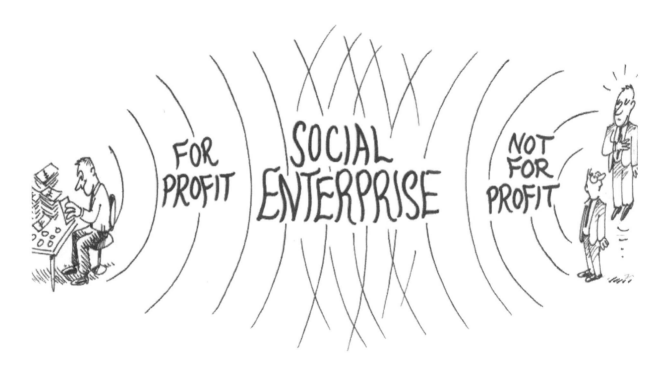

INTERFERENCE WAVES

FOR PROFIT

SOCIAL ENTERPRISE

NOT FOR PROFIT

Profit organizations and Non-profits can fuse their efforts and use all profits to expand non-profit activities, to create social enterprise

We earlier asked whether values did not resemble interference waves that create elegant patterns. We have asked why For-Profit organizations might not "interfere" with Non-Profit organizations and their purposes to form Social Enterprises, which both serve people and renew themselves by ploughing profits back into their efforts. Might consumers choose to buy not just the product but the character of the supplying organization? The world-wide success of The Body Shop, Interface Carpets, Desso, and Ben and Jerry's show that such appeals work well and customers are capable of thinking of more than just themselves. Moreover, enterprises whose appeal attracts customers can grow larger and larger while government supplied welfare hangs by a thread in many countries and is often slashed as a condition for the International Monetary Fund coming to a nation's aid and bailing it out. The problem with Non-profit is its small scale, its need to beg and only those with money can afford to be noble and rise above their fellows. The problem with For-profit enterprise is that all too easily it becomes an end itself. We need hybrids made of both. Few people can afford altruism for long. They can help others in the process of helping themselves.

❧

NEW ALLIANCES: 2. CONSUMERS WITH BEST PRACTICE COMPANIES

Which

awards the

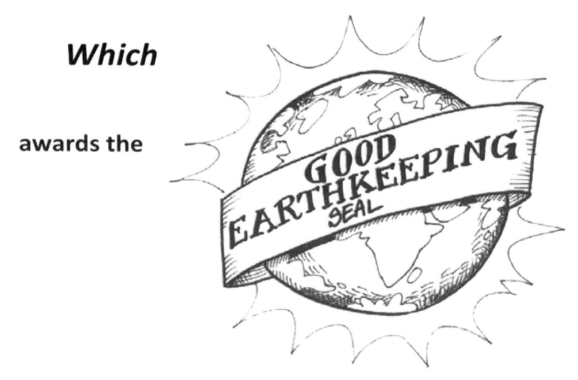

to IKEA

A FOR-PROFIT COMPANY WHOSE CORPORATE SOCIAL RESPONSIBILITY IS TESTIFIED TO BY A NON-PROFIT ADVOCATE OF A SUSTAINABLE ENVIRONMENT MAY APPEAL TO CONSUMERS. NO COMPANY IS PERFECT BUT MANY CAN SEEK TO DO BETTER, WITH HELP FROM THOSE WHO CARE AND THEIR ORGANIZATIONS.

Instead of always criticising companies it is often more effective to praise them, and praise from a non-profit champion of sustainability is praise indeed. This endorsement is imaginary but we do think that IKEA deserves this for its efforts. Nor do we have enough knowledge of WHICH? (short of supporting its aims.) Our point is a more general one, that awards to profit organizations from non-profits-with-a-cause is far more effective than any amount of advertising and contrived PR. That you have come up to the standards demanded by an advocacy organization while still making a profit so you could double the size of your operation or better is an important message to get over. It is a risk of course for the company seeking to meet the standard as it could fall short. And it is a risk for the non-profit which gains members by being whiter than white and untouchable by vulgar commerce! It really depends whether you want to improve operations or remain an immaculate purist. Companies should, in our view, admit in advance that mistakes will be made. IKEA will, on occasion, order a coffee table from someone who mistreats its carpenters. The real question is whether it then sanctions its errant supplier and learns from the experience. We should not certify that someone is perfect but that s/he is genuinely trying to improve and needs you to supply information to bring this about. Those eager to punish companies should reflect on the fact that not receiving a seal could soon become a punishment, especially if their competitors get one. Moreover, companies benefitted by such endorsement will do much to avoid it being revoked. Organized consumers on the Internet have great power. We urge that they come to realize this. Even identifying companies who do the least harm could be effective.

※

CAN PROFITS FUND PROGRESSIVE SOCIAL POLICIES? THE CASE OF UNILEVER

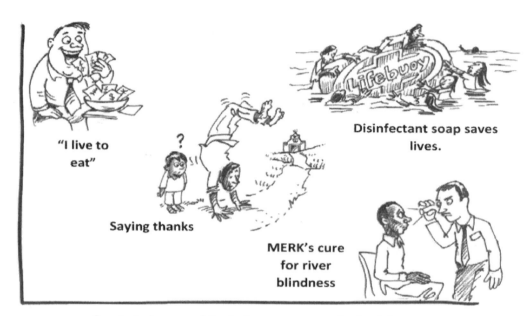

Me, myself, money and more

"I live to eat"

Saying thanks

Disinfectant soap saves lives.

MERK's cure for river blindness

Sustaining and helping your stakeholders

UNILEVER'S CAMPAIGN TO GET 2 MILLION CHILDREN PAST THEIR FIFTH BIRTHDAY IS SURELY SOMETHING CONSUMERS COULD SUPPORT WITH THEIR PURCHASES. MANY OF ITS PRODUCTS FIGHT DISEASE AND SAVE LIVES. THE COMPANY HELPS SUPPLY AND CONSERVE FRESH WATER BECAUSE BOTH PEOPLE AND ITS PRODUCTS NEED THIS.

Unilever, the Dutch and British consumer goods multinational company, is a supporter of the Conscious Capitalism movement. It owns Ben and Jerry's ice cream, which has designated itself a Benefit Corporation. Under the leadership of Paul Polman, it has distinguished itself in the area of corporate social responsibility by profiting (vertical dimension) while dedicating itself to the welfare of its stakeholders (lateral dimension). It leads other corporations in gender equality and actually pays female staff slightly more than men, perhaps because most customers are female. The illustration opposite shows what happens when profiting alone matters to a company (top left). Helping stakeholders can cost a company. MERK, the drug supplier, developed a successful cure for river blindness, but the Africans affected by this disease cannot afford to pay enough to profit MERK. It sells the drug at a loss.

Unilever runs a world campaign to save some of the two million children in the world who never reach their fifth birthday. The father walking on his hands to a Hindu shrine opposite is giving thanks for his child's fifth birthday. Unilever captured this authentic celebration on film. Most of the world's poor lack flush-toilets and Lifebuoy disinfectant soap plays a major part in fighting typhoid, cholera, dysentery and similar public health scourges, and the government helps sponsor the campaign. A film made by Unilever for pregnant mothers has healthy five-year olds thanking their pretend-mothers for always washing their hands and kitchen surfaces so carefully. This is certainly in the company's interests but it is much more than that. Over a million girls have joined Dove's campaign for female self-esteem. This is the point of what they buy to keep themselves attractive. The campaign stresses how diverse beauty can be and stresses its multiple forms. Unilever has created 1,000 "perfect villages" in Vietnam. It gives career advice to 114,000 women. It heads the Sustainability Indexes of both Dow Jones and Oxfam. It especially stresses its Sustainable Living Brands, which fight disease. £1 sterling invested in the company in 1986 would yield £86 today. No wonder Kraft-Heinz wanted to take it over and get those monies for shareholders alone!

MIGHT CONSUMERS BE WILLING TO BUY SOCIAL JUSTICE?

B&J HAS THE POLICY THAT WE HAVE INSCRIBED ON THE CARTON OF ICE-CREAM. WHY NOT TELL CONSUMERS, AND LET THEM BUY FAIRNESS? B&J, A SUBSIDIARY OF UNILEVER, IS A BENEFIT CORPORATION.

There are limits to what can be achieved by the re-distribution of incomes. To have private institutions allocate pay and then have public institutions taking it away from people who feel they have earned it, only to give it to people who earn very little and have fewer skills, is far from being an ideal or effective arrangement. It creates agonizing dilemmas for those not quite good enough to earn a decent income and not quite bad enough to need a hand-out. Those with big incomes are politically powerful enough to avoid taxes by hundreds of devices and the system itself needs expensive lawyers which only the rich can afford. The code has thousands of loop-holes inserted by special interests. Avoiding taxes has become a way of life. It is much cheaper to collect from those who cannot afford to litigate and compromise with those who can. The results are manifestly unjust. One countervailing force is to pressure companies into much more equal pay systems, instead of having those with most power reward themselves and their friends. One solution is pre-distribution. Ben and Jerry's has one of the most equal pay systems and has long been a highly successful company, backing progressive social causes and even featuring the faces of missing children. It is also a Benefit Corporation. The ratio of top to bottom wages is only 5-1, see the illustration. The Fair's Fair flavour is our own invention as is the public proclamation of this ratio which you can read about on the internet but is not yet used to attract consumers. The company is now a subsidiary of Unilever which spends lavishly in helping women world-wide who do much of the shopping for its products. It is a supporter of the Conscious Capitalism movement. If consumers want a fairer pay-structure, they can get it by asking companies to reveal their pay ratios and rewarding what they believe is fair to women and others.

CAN WE BUY A BETTER WORLD? THE CHARACTER OF CORPORATIONS.

We made this ad up but it seems to us a possibility, something we could at least try

A recent survey found that 52% of Americans over 40 take Aspirin regularly as a preventative of coronary diseases. Many cardiologists recommend this. We reckon this could help you as an individual. But there is an additional reason for taking Just Aspirin and helping people who really need it. For many people Just Aspirin means aspirin pure and simple with none of the lies and the flummery which pretend that one kind is better than another and which force you to pay for being deceived. We make aspirin too, no better and no worse than the others, but while we make it we build a community, bring hope to thousands who never had hope before. And we're making our part of town a liveable place again with safe streets, decent homes and industrious people. Come and see us & you may get fewer headaches. To us our brand means a just society with social justice and help for all. Why not try to reach beyond pills to people. We need each other, right?

There is much recent fuss about corporate social responsibility and how businesses should do more than make profits, but CSR which is just an add-on and another form of PR, is all very well when we can afford it but is the first to go when we cannot. It is not the answer. What we need is an orientation to customers and to society which is part of a shared strategy to elevate all relevant stakeholders. We need people to buy our aspirin because we help the poor, the disabled and the otherwise jobless, because we send their brighter children to college and give them a better start in life. It does not have to be aspirin. It can be stationery, pens, school notebooks, envelopes – anything with the space that allows us to explain what we are doing and why. We need nothing less than a new alliance between consumers and suppliers. Many objects for sale are routine and prosaic but this allows us to find additional reasons to buy them. We need a society where all are industrious, all contribute to a fairer deal, where values are put ahead of everything else. To be poor is first and foremost to have nothing to give. It is that we have to change. We all need to contribute and just receiving welfare and hand-outs is dispiriting and not the answer. Attempts at self-help must be rewarded, much as we reward amputees for climbing hills.

New Alliances 3. Getting online communities on-side

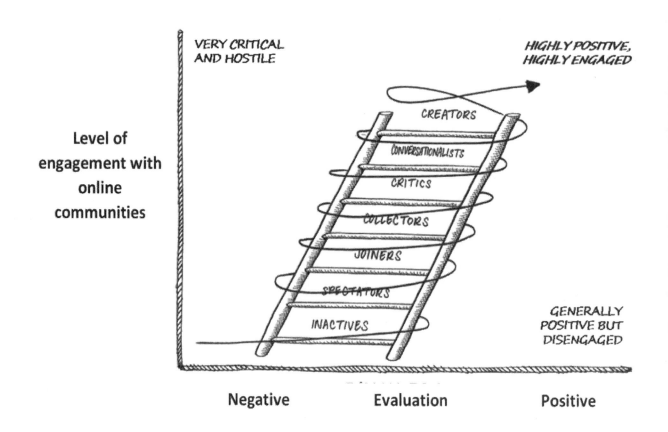

VERY CRITICAL AND HOSTILE

HIGHLY POSITIVE, HIGHLY ENGAGED

Level of engagement with online communities

CREATORS

CONVERSATIONALISTS

CRITICS

COLLECTORS

JOINERS

SPECTATORS

INACTIVES

GENERALLY POSITIVE BUT DISENGAGED

Negative   Evaluation   Positive

Companies should encourage online communities who speak to them of social responsibility and report breaches

Companies are more and more in touch with social media and online communities, commenting on the conduct of that company. Many of these are potential customers, suppliers, employees and partners. These persons are more or less engaged with the conduct of a company and more or less positive or negative in their evaluations of it. It is clearly in the interests of the company that its online audience becomes more engaged and more positive over time. If the company is turning people off, then it needs to know this. Charlene Li and Josh Bernoff have created a Social Technographics Ladder to assess a company's credibility and social reputation. If the online participants are angry then at least they care and this could be important. It is important that companies learn how to improve. Bad reactions from "out there" are early warning signs. If you wait for profits to fall it could be too late. The labels near the bottom are largely unengaged and on the negative side, inactives and spectators. The joiners and the collectors show medium interest, while critics, provided they are constructive, can be quite valuable and show strong signs of being engaged. Conversation may be among the most valuable forms of communication, since either party can change the subject at will and address what is best and worst about a company. It is often effective to pay NGOs to evaluate you. They are frequently passionate about their cause and earning their praise is a high hurdle. At the highest level of all, you co-create with those who care most. LEGO, for example, sells robots made from their bricks and children create and exchange computer programmes on how to activate these. The company presides over this market place. It could sue the children-inventors but knows better! Co-creation is the strongest bond of all and has the capacity to last a life-time. Such developments bring social marketing ever closer. We need to be able to reward companies for their contributions to our communities so that they profit.

∽

THE CHANGING FACE OF MARKETING: EVOLVING PARADIGMS

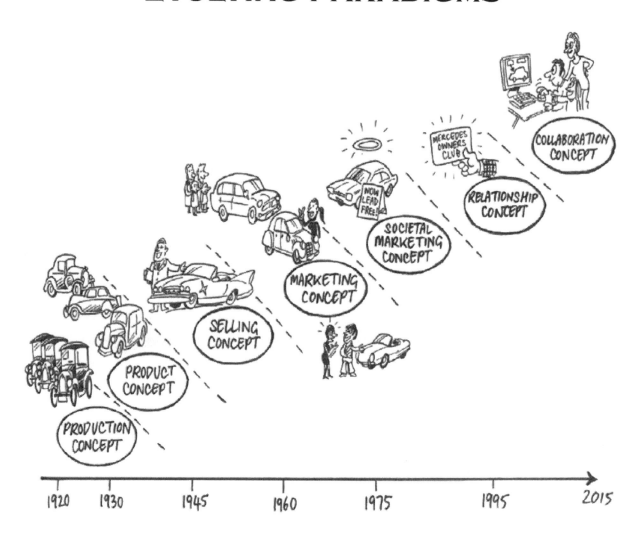

WHY NOT TRY ACTUALLY *HELPING* CUSTOMERS!

The Finnish professor, Christian Gronroos, has completed these successive stages in the evolution of marketing paradigms. At the earliest stage was the Production Concept. Anything produced by mass manufacturing was so much cheaper than hand-crafted products that they sold at once. This followed the Product Concept, exemplified by the Model T Ford which even workers could afford. You could have "any colour you liked so long as it was black." Standardization facilitated rock bottom prices. As the economy filled up with cheaply manufactured goods, there arose the Selling Concept. Products being very much the same, competitive advantage moved to those who pushed theirs the hardest and persuaded customers to buy them. This widened over time into the Marketing Concept, famous for its mix of enticements, branding, advertising, point of sale, service and image. From here concerns were raised as to whether the society benefitted. Was the car cleaner, did it save on fuel? What were its levels of emission? Was its owner socially responsible? This is the Societal Marketing Concept. At a further stage, the Relationship Concept, the buyers and users start to organize and feed-back to the company their agreed opinions on the value and the quality of the products and services. At the highest stage, Collaboration Concept, all producers and buyers collaborate to create the product. This is most often seen in business-to-business relationships. What is sold is the product idea yet to be developed and a team made up of members of both companies work together to achieve this. The supplier may sell a potential solution, the result of a product being successfully installed, manned and operating effectively. Those who have co-created forge close and lasting bonds. They share the same fate.

❦

Only for-profit companies have the power to scale up

It is large corporations (like Unilever, Johnson and Johnson, Whole Foods and UPS) which can change capitalism by scaling up their current activities. Women, who do most of the shopping, have massive latent powers. Just 5% of their numbers could change everything.

Michael Porter has started four Non-Governmental Organizations. When as a business strategist he encountered a problem outside business - as he then thought - he would start an NGO to take on the problem. Then it dawned on him that NGOs were too small and perhaps too many for the funds available and were all begging for spare change from those who were making money. The good ideas had too little money and many of those with money were bereft of good ideas. It was essential to put the good ideas where the money was. He came up with the notion of shared strategy, close to the thesis of this book. The strategy of wealth creation should include the health, wealth and development of employees, the nurturing of suppliers, the empowerment of customers and the sustainability of the environment. It is only by turning all these to profit that you can scale-up. If it is profitable to skill employees, grow suppliers and sustain the environment, then there is no limit to the extent that social impact can be scaled up by private enterprise. Profitability becomes the flame that assures ascent. Funding NGOs assumes business cannot do it, but it can. Many businesses now hire NGOs to monitor whether the social impacts they seek to make are genuine. If the NGO is passionate and has high standards all the better. It will hold your feet to the fire. The for-profit company will be held to its promises by those most dedicated to the public good. The government could lavish praise on companies with the best records and award these contracts. The media could publish their attainments and attract customers.

❧

c) GOVERNMENT AS REFEREE, COMMANDER OR COACH

The Government referees and defines fair play

Degree of government intervention

GOVERNMENTS CAN INFLUENCE AN ECONOMY IN SEVERAL WAYS. THE REFEREE IS UNPOPULAR, THE WINNING COACH IS OFTEN ADORED.

In this section we will see that governments in the world play three roles. The role most familiar in the West sees the government as a Referee of a fair contest between private enterprises. Here the government is supposedly neutral and impartial and should not distort market forces. The Referee is depicted at top left blowing his whistle. As any football or baseball fan will tell you, Referees or umpires are rarely popular, hence the hail of missiles. Governments of this kind tend to be cursed by all sides. The doctrine of strong government influence is French, (see the General), and is known as Dirigisme. This is much criticised as oppressive, yet the Chinese boast of a Socialist Market-Driven economy and this has performed spectacularly well, as have many of the Pacific Rim nations, most with strong government guidance. What seems to work very well is Government as a Coach, not spelling out what companies must do but generally encouraging the best of them to do better. Coaches of winning teams are popular, so much so that the Government of Singapore has never lost an election. We are not always honest with ourselves on this topic. The USA has a massive military-industrial complex and the biggest command economy in the world by far, dedicated to space and weaponry. As we shall see, its basic research funding has played a decisive role in the success of Apple among others. Coach governments, who admit this role, also pay teachers very well, stress education and give priority to knowledge intensive products over simpler ones. They target "horizontal" technologies that cut across industry and "feed" other technologies by raising their intelligence. Governments also control infrastructure and spending on this can be very effective. We will also consider what government might do about welfare and poverty generally.

&

GOVERNING BY ARTFUL NUDGES: LIBERTARIAN-PATERNALISM

THE GOVERNMENT AS THE "CHOICE ARCHITECT" GIVING YOU INFORMATION YOU ARE FREE TO IGNORE IF YOU SO DECIDE, BUT IS WISE AND PARENTAL

We earlier criticised the attempt by the social sciences to predict and control behaviour. It is not possible fortunately, but were it so, it would herald a totalitarian degree of power by controllers over controlees. The very aspiration is unworthy. But there is now a new science of influence, wherein government or private enterprise nudges the person in the direction desired. This action, according to Richard H Thaler and Cass R. Sunstein, is a mix of paternalism and libertarianism. It is paternal in the sense that someone in authority is advising you on what you should do and it is libertarian in the sense that you are free to ignore the advice if you wish to and the choices may be usefully clarified. Authorities in government and elsewhere are choice architects. They display choices and describe in significant ways. They may wish customers to choose the options best for their health and welfare or they may give prominence to options more profitable to suppliers. In the image opposite, Uncle Sam is nudging a girl to choose the food option which will lead her to be slimmer, more active and lead a longer life untroubled by the many diseases triggered by obesity and the loneliness of being unattractive. Since he sets the rules he is potentially able to inform her of the long-term value of the two options, notwithstanding her impulse to reach for the hamburger. Does nudging her reduce her liberty? Not if she has fifteen more years of life, not if she is free to ignore the advice and choose the fattier option, not if she is slim enough anyway and needs to put on weight, not if the true information allows her to choose more wisely, not if her self-discipline and impulse control is enhanced. The simple process of maximizing the number of choices does not work in the way its proponents claim. People can process only so much information before they stop choosing, especially where their commitment is low and they have not the time. Providing choice is also more expensive, with many smaller lots and the poor may be able to afford less food as a result. Some companies have made great gains by reducing choice to fewer yet clearer and better alternatives as in the case of Lidl and Aldi markets. What works best is a fusion of advice and free choice with the choices set out and clearly labelled. In the case of organ donation, this saves so many lives that people should opt out, with silence implying consent.

Was the Arms' Race the Secret of America's economic power?

Every improved spear needs a better shield. Every improved shield demands a better spear. High-tech is subsidized by the military industrial complex.

The Chinese have a lot less trouble with paradoxes and dilemmas than we do. They see these not as an attack on rationality but as a clever way of getting two contrasting values to stimulate each other. The word for 'dilemma' in Chinese characters is 'Spear and Shield', see top of illustration. There is indeed a dilemma from moment to moment in any battle as to whether you should strike with your spear or parry with your shield. On the other hand, no sensible warrior goes into conflict without both instruments so they are essentially complementary, like attack and defence. There is a story attached to these combined characters. There was once a maker of weapons who famously claimed that the spear he had designed could penetrate the strongest shield. He did a roaring trade. He next claimed that he had made a shield which could protect against the sharpest spear. His trade picked up again. Those who had bought the spear worried about how to protect themselves from it in another's hands. Those who had bought the shield now wondered whether their existing spear was strong enough for a counter-attack. It was really an early manifestation of the arms' race, or the role of competition in spurring cooperation and vice versa. Note that once again the system is circular with customers going from line to line indefinitely. Each improvement necessitates the next one. We are now on the verge of a military robot race. We suggest that the arms-race dating from World War 1 and lasting for over a century, is the secret of America's economic power.

∽ଚ

THE ROLE OF THE FEDERAL GOVERNMENT IN APPLE'S INNOVATION

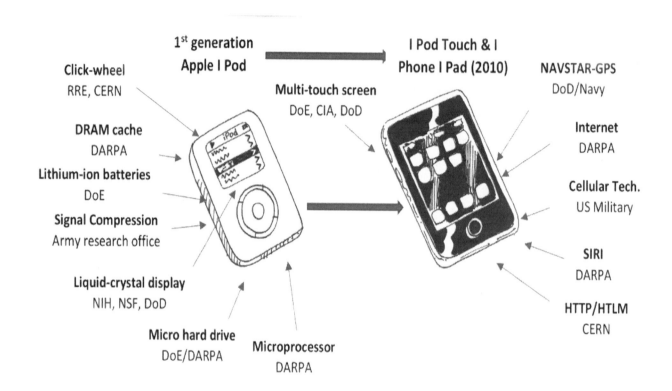

APPLE IS SUPPOSED TO BE A GLOBAL SAGA OF THE "TWO STEVES IN THE GARAGE." PRIVATE ENTERPRISE STRIKES AGAIN. AS WE SEE ABOVE, EVERY NOVEL FEATURE OF THE APPLE iPOD WAS TAKEN FROM THE BASIC RESEARCH OF GOVERNMENTS.

The USA has long claimed that it is almost entirely inspired by the brilliance of its entrepreneurs and that the state is bureaucratic, hidebound and an impediment to private genius. The story of Steve Jobs and Steve Wozniak in their garage is close to the founding mythology of Apple. The Federal government has nothing to do with such spectacular success and must be kept in check lest its dead hand slows progress. But the reality is very, very different according to economist Mariana Mazzucato. Opposite she traces the main features of the Apple iPod and its subsequent development into the iPhone. In every case the basic research came from *The Entrepreneurial State* as her book is called, and the defence-oriented largesse of the Federal Government, from which Apple has withheld taxes by keeping its profits abroad. The illustration reveals that DARPA (Defence Advanced Research Projects Agency) provided the Micro hard drive and the DRAM (Dynamic random-access memory) cache in the iPod, and the SIRI (Intelligent Personal Assistant) and provided the internet to the iPhone. The Lithium batteries came from the Department of Energy, as did the Multi-touch screen. The Department of Defence helped develop the Liquid Crystal Display, the NAVSTAR and the Multi-touch screen. CERN, (the European Council for Nuclear Research), developed the Click Wheel and HTTP/HTML (Hypertext Transfer Protocol/ Hypertext Mark-up Language).

The truth of the matter is that the American economy is a vast beneficiary of government defence spending and the economy has grown fastest through arming allies in two world wars and the Cold War arms' race of which space exploration was an offshoot. One of the only subjects that liberals and conservatives can agree on, is government defence spending and for decades America has had the largest command economy in the world, a form of socialism dedicated to defeating socialism! This has subsidized high tech in the cause of protecting the nation. It was an industrial strategy in all but name. It was this strategy that filled weapons and communications full of knowledge and drove the basic research which Apple commercialized. So far from "oppressing" industry, government agencies convene forums and do much early development work which it then hands over to the likes of Apple, which declines to help the tax-payer and borrows to pay shareholders.

D). HOW WE NEED TO THINK DIFFERENTLY
ARE MICRO-CHIPS MORE VALUABLE THAN POTATO CHIPS?

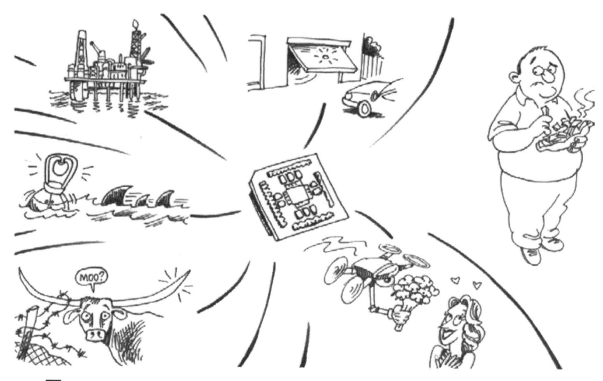

THE VALUE OF PRODUCTS IN NOT CONVEYED BY THEIR PRICE ALONE. SOME PRODUCTS LIKE MICROCHIPS RENDER OTHER PRODUCTS FAR MORE VALUABLE AND RAMIFY THOUGH AN ECONOMY. EMERGING NATIONS OFTEN SPECIALIZE IN THESE.

According to economic orthodoxy, values are subjective but become objective when a price is put on them. It follows that $100 worth of microchips are equal to $100 worth of potato chips and it is for buyers not suppliers to register these prices. No product is inherently better than another until it finds its price. Except that this misses a vital point. Suppose a nation excels at producing microchips, what the Japanese call "the rice of industry", since they nourish it. If ranchers put chips in the horns of cattle in Texas, they can trace all animals in the herd. Buoys in Australia have chips that can locate sharks at a distance and sound the alarm. A microchip will tell how much oil compared with water is left in a well so recovery has been greatly enhanced. A garage door can be opened remotely and a drone can be guided to a customer. In short, micro-chips not only animate and inform a thousand other products but greatly enhance their effectiveness along with the price customers are willing to pay. Some products make other products more intelligent and useful as a total system. This is not confined to microchips. Number controlled machine tools make other tools that help run a factory. Industrial robots, specialized robots, liquid crystal displays, universal joints, automated production processes, metal ceramics, metal alloys, photovoltaic cells, lithium batteries etc. are all drivers within human systems. The most intelligent industrial strategy is to sponsor and target products that do the most for other products and the economy generally. Every dollar put into microchips could boost our brain power. Every dollar put into potato chips only boosts the size of your stomach. Most East Asian countries ignored economic advice from the West and went straight for the cutting edge of electronics, not labour intensive as much as knowledge intensive. The real competitive advantage lies between our ears. Products with knowledge intensity have more potential than other products. They teach each other and they teach us. Favouring knowledge intensity does not obstruct free markets. There is more freedom at the top of the knowledge ladder than at its base. Knowledge conveys meaning and meaning motivates. If I give you potato chips for money then I can have the money or the chips but not both. But if I convey knowledge to you electronically I give the knowledge and I keep it. We are in a new place.

WHAT ARE THE TRUE VALUE OF INFRASTRUCTURE PROJECTS?

WHAT IS THE VALUE OF UP-TO-DATE INFRASTRUCTURE? GERMANY AND JAPAN, WHO HAD TO REBUILD THEIR INFRASTRUCTURE AFTER WORLD WAR II, BOTH EXPERIENCED BOOMS. INFRASTRUCTURE TOUCHES MILLIONS OF PEOPLE IN SCORES OF WAYS.

What does infrastructure and its improvement contribute to an economy? There are reasons to believe the effect is very powerful. Emerging nations have very high growth rates in part, it is said, because the first bridge across a river, replacing ferries, can increase people traffic by 1,000%. A road increases the price of land next to it many times over and the acreage is considerable. Is it a coincidence that Germany and Japan, which lost much of their infrastructure in World War II, both enjoyed economic miracles in the wake of it? Modern infrastructure is much more efficient than old. Put utilities beneath large curb stones at the road's edge and you may never have to dig up the road again! There is also strong bias against governments and their expenditures so that "less government" as a political demand, ends up reducing investments in infrastructure, leading to J.K. Galbraith's "private affluence and public squalor", with pricey cars ruined by pot-holes. But perhaps the greatest handicap comes from difficulty in counting the gains from infrastructure development and the sustainability of cities in general. The picture opposite follows KPMG's efforts to discover the True Value of the Dutch Railway system. What should we count? The fact that car traffic now moves faster, saving thousands of people twenty minutes off their commuting time and raising time worked, that there are fewer cars on the road and hence less pollution, that admissions to hospitals for respiratory diseases are down 25%, that children can now play in the open air, that there is more space for shoppers to park and higher sales result? Then of course there are the wages paid to public workers which enter the economy very quickly and then taxes collected. Were we to take such estimates seriously we might realize that infrastructure is a priceless boon for most nations. It is known, for example, that every additional tax inspector pays the department five times his/her salary but Congress still insists that staff be cut back! It robs us all.

Values forming relationships of synergy

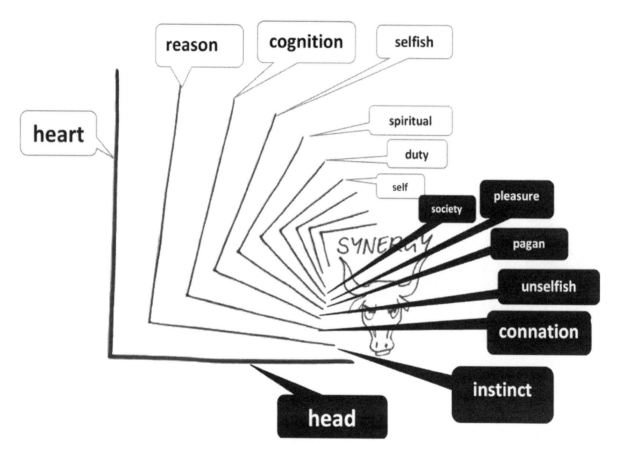

Abraham Maslow studied outstanding individuals of his age and some historical figures. He came to the conclusion illustrated above.

Much of the inspiration for this book and our entire life's work comes from this passage in the work of Abraham Maslow. The American psychiatrist was looking at healthy and creative persons who had actualized their own potentials and capacities. He noticed that, unlike many other people, they had succeeded in bringing these into fine syntheses. He called this synergy, from the Greek, *syn-ergo* - to work together - and conflict between them disappears because they join together for the same ends and point to the same conclusions. Certain values in just the right proportions suddenly fuse and grow. The excerpt below comes from *Motivation and Personality* (1954).

"The age-old opposition between heart and head, reason and instinct, or cognition and connation was seen to disappear in healthy people where they became synergic rather than antagonists... The dichotomy between selfishness and unselfishness disappears... because in principle every act is both selfish and unselfish ...Our subjects are simultaneously very spiritual and very pagan and sensual. Duty cannot be contrasted with pleasure or work with play where duty is pleasure, when work is play. Similar findings have been reached for kindness-ruthlessness, concreteness-abstractness, acceptance-rebellion, serious-frivolous, mystic-realistic, active-passive, lust-love, Eros-Agape...and a thousand philosophical dilemmas are discovered to have more than two horns, or paradoxically no horns at all."

◈

THE SUPREME HUMAN VALUE EMERGING FROM THIS BOOK IS SYNERGY...

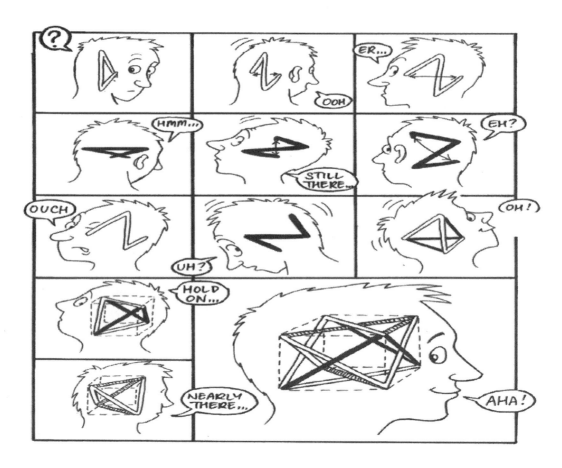

CONSTRUCTING A WHOLE WHICH IS MORE THAN THE SUM-OF-ITS-PARTS IS THE SECRET OF WEALTH CREATION AND IMPROVED RELATIONSHIPS.

W e have seen in much of this book that the secret lies in relationships of ideas and people, but these must have a particular quality of fitting finely together and working with each other to produce wealth and value. The illustration opposite is from Buckminster Fuller, architect, designer and systems theorist. It begins with a white and black triangle, both bent into the shape of a helix (the template of life). If you combine the helices you get a tetrahedron which is then combined with another to create a cube. You now have a stable structure with a third dimension and is a unit of architecture, see his geodesic dome. It has moved to a higher level of complexity and is stronger, more stable and more resilient. This combination is much more than the sum of its four triangles and is unpredictable from those parts. Synergy takes many forms, from the fusion of seemingly opposed values, to materials science wherein chrome, nickel and steel are incredibly stronger than any one metal or all of these added up and they stop a jet engine melting. Values can combine too. This is more than a mental exercise; it is an architectural innovation which alters our shared reality. It is we who socially construct ideas and must then live with the consequences.

Values and relationships: helping and healing

"… Our eyes met … I kid you not. All the drugs I've taken, all that steamy sex, all those highs can't beat that moment, and we were not even touching."

Bill Tolliver was admitted to the Delancey Street Foundation, a halfway house in San Francisco for mostly addicted ex-felons. He had bitten two holes in his tongue and nearly drowned in his own blood. Yet he recovered and over the years became the unofficial "high priest" in charge of most celebrations and much of the therapy. He told me the following story.

"I have also wanted to change people. I used to do it by manipulation and that's hard work! I would exhaust myself and them and it rarely lasted; but recently I've learned to do it by the lightest of touches, by my 'finger-tips' as it were, and some force greater than my own, greater than both of us, takes over. There was a young woman in my 'tribe' (family unit), gorgeous to look at but with a drug habit and career that had veered from one catastrophe to the next. Her father had just died and we were sitting with her, trying to pick up the pieces. She felt very guilty. Their last quarrel had been about her drug-taking and stealing. She was angry with her father for leaving her alone. She was weeping by the hour. When I sensed the grief was almost out of her, I said softly. "but there must have been good times too, tell us about those." She thought for a moment and began to tell us; with every memory her voice grew stronger and her eyes brighter and she was smiling through her tears. Finally, she jumped to her feet, kissed all of us on the cheek and turned to leave the room, looking radiant. "Now you know what you must do in this family," I told her. "Your father is dead but we have seen him in your spirit, in your smile and in your bearing. You must live among us and any family you create, so that when you die, they will recall you in the same way with all that love inside." She paused and looked back at me. Our eyes met. I kid you not, all the drugs I've taken, all the steamy sex, all those towering highs can't beat that moment and we were not even touching."

PARADOXES ABOUND: THE DIALECTIC DANCE OF OPPOSITES

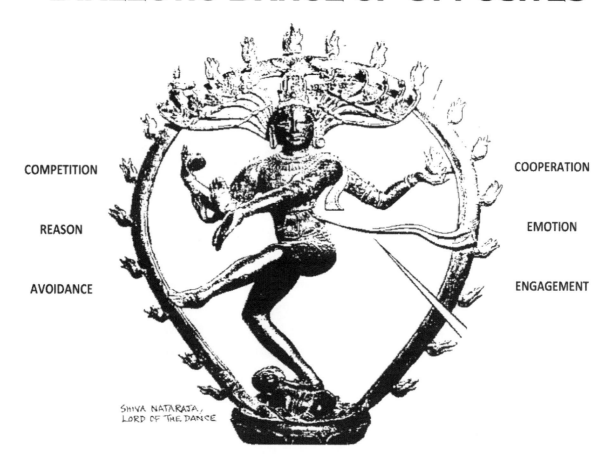

COMPETITION

REASON

AVOIDANCE

COOPERATION

EMOTION

ENGAGEMENT

SHIVA NATARAJA, LORD OF THE DANCE

ARE PARADOXES FORMS OF NORMAL DISCOURSE AND LANGUAGE? DOES DIVERSITY AND PLURALISM MAKE PARADOX UNAVOIDABLE? IS IT A LENS TO VIEW REALITY?

Professor Linda Putman sees economic and social discourses as a "dance of opposites", illustrated by Shiva, the dancing god of Hindu religion. Putman is setting out to build a language of paradox. This is not something strange or exceptional. It is the "new normal". We have to move away from treating language opposites as ruptures in the reasoning process. We must accept and embrace the plurality of perspectives. The structures of human discourse are paradoxical owing to varied experiences of living. Tension, struggle and clashes are routine, not abnormal. We live in a world of complexity and rapid change where our expectations are less often fulfilled and surprise is endemic. Paradox is a lens through which to view reality. We must embrace both polar ends of dimensions and have these engage each other constructively in a search for new unities. Among classic paradoxes are Cooperation vs. Competition, Reason vs. Emotion, and Avoidance vs. Engagement. Stories entertain us by serial crises among values and protagonists and would bore us otherwise. These collisions are resolved by some means or another. Social reality is dialectical and consists of an interplay of connected opposites. The seeds of resolution lie in dialogue. We must learn to manage conflict by understanding that both sides are true and must be included. Competition helps to differentiate us. Cooperation helps to join us, but it is genuine differences that must be joined. We have an inherent tendency to favour one pole and think simplistically. The answer is not meeting half-way, but finding a unity that enhances both values. If you have competed and come up with a powerful idea you can all cooperate around this. If you can avoid infuriating your opponent you can engage her more successfully. Emotion can alert you to a shoddy argument but examine that emotion reasonably and make feelings Reason's friend. The dialectics of dancing opposites promote discovery, spur innovation and help to transcend conflict, while leading to larger truths. Values infuse one another and become a source of learning.

❧

Dynamic equilibrium

WE EXPLOIT YET WE EXPLORE AND THE EXPLOITATION PAYS FOR THE EXPLORATION. GLOBALISM VIES WITH LOCALISM, FAILURE INFORMS SUCCESS, AS TENSIONS ARE RECONCILED. WE VEER TO ONE END. ONLY TO RETURN TO EQUILIBRIUM.

Wendy Smith, Marianne Lewis and Michael L Tushman are among a number of academics who insist that creating wealth is paradoxical, with seemingly opposed values finely tuned to a peak of perfection. Innovation, especially, is highly challenging and consists of associating and connecting meaningfully what was not joined before and was hitherto far apart or even opposed. Paradoxical tensions are reconciled by management strategies and wealth is generated by such fusions. For example, any viable globalism must engage with local differences, and shareholders must engage with the stakeholders they need to run a business successfully. Where this engagement succeeds there will be more not less for shareholders to gain. We need to exploit but also to explore and find more opportunities. We need to grow long-term but avoid being floored by short-term crises. In the illustration opposite, the acrobatic contestants are competing with each other while cooperating to avoid collision and make a show of their coordination. Each is different and yet their performance is unified. The more dynamic one is, the harder it is to retain equilibrium, yet the more spectacular is the feat, the more the audience marvels and pays; success is built on periodic failure followed by improvement. What we essentially have is a dance of opposites and it becomes essential to embrace both ends. Paradox is a lens for managing the conflict which naturally arises from different life-experiences and perceptions. Like the skateboarders opposite, we need to avoid striking each other, yet this can only happen if we are fully engaged. We need both the clarity which comes from polarization and the ambiguity which comes from fusion. A useful vehicle for this is the narrative. All narratives move from crisis to crisis and would not be enjoyable unless they created excitement within us. Will the two protagonists win the contest? Will the risks they take be rewarded? Will showing off doom them? Has the crowd thrilled by the spectacle and the danger really come to witness an accident? The scene is full of irony.

LEADERSHIP AND THE EXPERIENCE OF A CRUCIBLE IN YOUR PAST LIFE

"It was as if I was coming home to a place I'd never been before..."
Bill George

GREAT LEADERS HAVE HAD A MAJOR ISSUE IN THEIR PAST LIVES, A DILEMMA THAT STILL CHALLENGES THEM. THEIR ENERGIES ARE THROWN INTO THE TASK OF RECONCILING THIS AND ANYTHING THAT REMINDS THEM OF THIS.

It was Warren Bennis who noted that what set great leaders aside from their less distinguished peers was a "crucible" in their past lives, a traumatic event or challenge to their resilience as people, which they had withstood yet had shaped their outlook on life. They were re-fighting that past engagement in how they conducted themselves. In a crucible hot metals are forged. The crucible must have heat-withstanding powers or it will melt. The metals often form a new alloy or compound which has qualities that are far more than its ingredients, a much stronger integrity or bond. It is no discourtesy to Warren to say that in part he talked about himself, since he traced the authenticity of great leaders to that source. They expressed what they deeply believed and what they had actually experienced. He was a Jewish working-class boy from the Bronx, who joined the US army in 1943, was its youngest American officer in combat while still in his teens and won a Bronze Star for gallantry and a Purple Heart for serious wounds in battle. He counselled President Kennedy before his fortieth birthday and three other Presidents. His life-long opposition to command-and-control leadership and his fierce dedication to democratic participation expressed his response to fascism and the Holocaust.

Bill George, ex-CEO of Medtronic, and now professor at the Harvard Business School, regarded Warren as his mentor. While still in his twenties he lost his mother and his fiancé to premature deaths. He never got over it but it shaped his leadership. He tried to redeem a promise to his father that he would head a major corporation, but nearing the top of the heap at Honeywell, he felt empty and despairing. He opted to be the vice president of a much smaller company, Medtronic, maker of pace-makers and defibrillators for the human heart. "It was like coming home to a place I'd never been before." On the face of it, it was a demotion. He took headship of the company and grew it from $1 billion to over $60 billion, redeeming his promise to his father and making the trauma of his early adulthood a lot less common experience for others. Medtronic hands out medallions to excellent employees, featuring patients rising from beds. It counts the extra years of life it has given patients and accepts moving tributes.

E). HOW WE NEED TO ACT DIFFERENTLY

ALIBABA, PLATFORM COMPANIES & SOCIAL JUSTICE

ALIBABA HAS SET UP A SYSTEM OF FAIR, HONEST, FAST TRADING WITH ANY CONFLICTS SWIFTLY ARBITRATED AND RECONCILED. THE CHINESE MIDDLE CLASS DESERVE A BREAK AS DO THEIR CONSUMERS IN GENERAL.

The record of platform companies, where buyers and sellers are brought together on a single Internet platform to trade freely, has been pretty patchy. eBay was pushed out of China, Airbnb has had its share of scandals. Uber over-works and under-pays its drivers, some of whom have killed themselves when pay was suddenly reduced. There remains one outstanding example not only of the biggest initial public offering in the history of Wall Street, but of social justice for Chinese, middle-class consumers and small traders. Alibaba, created by Jack Ma, originally a Chinese English teacher who learned the language by helping tourists, received $42.7 billion for his company. This was despite his statement that customers came first, his employees second and shareholders third. If shareholders stand to gain it seems they tolerate Asian capitalism. Alibaba in the famous story watched the forty thieves store their stolen treasure in a cave, which at the words "Open Sesame!" yielded sight of vast treasure within. It was the same with Jack's company Alibaba. On Singles Day in China, $27 billion or more is spent on 11/11 (November 11th). In the early stages of China's rapid growth, exports of capital goods got priority, consumers were relatively neglected. Communism has always praised the proletariat and criticized its bourgeois middle class, who were relatively neglected. Alibaba put an end to that, helped by the 2008 Recession, and has hugely boosted domestic consumption in the PRC. It guarantees the promises of all suppliers, however small, and will deny access to any who cheat, which in effect ruins them. It allows customers to post complaints which, when remedied, are removed. It assures prompt payment and one-day delivery of goods. It has its own in-house arbiters of any disputes, which are faster and fairer than Chinese courts. It makes millions of relationships more equal than before.

ဆ

KICKSTARTER, THE CROWDFUNDER, RECENTLY BECAME A B CORPORATION

IN CROWDFUNDING, THE INVESTORS CONTRIBUTE BEFORE THE PRODUCT IS LAUNCHED AND THE FOUNDER CAN THEREFORE DESCRIBE AN IDEAL PRODUCT OR SERVICE S/HE WOULD LIKE TO CREATE, JOINING WITH CO-CREATORS AND "MIDWIVES" TO MAKE IT HAPPEN. KICKSTARTER LIVES UP TO ITS NAME AND MOVES YOU UP THE MOUNTAIN.

Prominent among crowdfunding platforms is Kickstarter, one of the best-known B Corporations on the internet. The idea of the Benefit Corporation sprang from the heads of four Californian entrepreneurs who wished to create a new kind of business corporation with a mission to all stakeholders, not just shareholders. A company creates its own by-laws which pledge it to serve all those who have contributed to the company's existence, especially the community formed by the company and the community surrounding it. Running the company for profitability alone is expressly forbidden, and contributors could sue and leaders be dismissed were this to be attempted. There are over 1,000 such corporations in the USA and more than 400 in Europe. The founders are chiefly concerned with the task of certifying what benefits have been delivered and the B Lab does this certifying. Some B Corporations are certified by State laws, so criteria vary. The fear is that loads of "green-wash" will obliterate fine distinctions and claims will not be credible. Sustainability could become a band-wagon. Kick-starter has made its name by crowdfunding projects, mostly by artists, writers and musicians and getting more than a third of its projects enough investment money to be launched. Projects say how much money they need for a launch and use the platform to appeal, with the platform taking 15%. On a world-scale, crowdfunding has more than doubled each year. The prospect of crowdfunding and B-corporations forming an alliance could be highly significant, giving socially ambitious projects the impetus illustrated opposite, especially when specialising in sustainable businesses. Social enterprises need a kick-start, not simply gaining investors but suppliers, customers, partners and employees.

CROWDFUNDING COMES TO PRIME-TIME TELEVISION

ONE WAY TO DEMONSTRATE THAT BUSINESS CAN SAVE OUR PLANET AND HAS A SOCIAL PURPOSE, NOT JUST PRIVATE GAIN, IS TO MAKE A TELEVISED SHOW OUT OF SUCH EFFORTS. PROMISES MADE PUBLICLY WHEN A PRODUCT IS LAUNCHED ARE MORE LIKELY TO ENDURE LIKE A MARRIAGE.

It is surely just a matter of time before crowd-funding moves from the Internet to prime-time TV. We have imagined a biodegradable, disposable shopping bag made of potato starch that might even feed rather than kill marine life, nurturing them and the environment instead. Campaigns to help sick children on the BBC raise millions. Here viewers would buy shares in noble causes and gain both morally and financially where these were successful. Yet the main reason for these celebrations is to raise the consciousness of the public that relatively developed economies like the European Union members and the UK must innovate or die. Nearly all conventional products can be made more cheaply in East Asia. What we must learn is non-stop innovation with generations of new products following each other as science progresses. It is NOT the survival of the fittest but the Survival of the Finest Fit, see left of illustration. We must fit into the ecology of the world. Sir David Attenborough has already shown how we are destroying the ocean with even arctic fish ingesting plastic which breaks into tiny pieces but never disappears. We need to arouse public support and get shareholders to support environmental goals. The big advantage of such displays is to turn our consumer orientation as a culture to ethical goals, so we can "buy" the kind of world we want. We need major sums of money to make a difference, along with consumer and investor support for such campaigns. We need a society where the nobility of your aspirations gets the support it deserves. The image opposite is consistent with The Daily Mail's campaign against plastic waste.

PLASTIC IN THE RIGHT PLACE

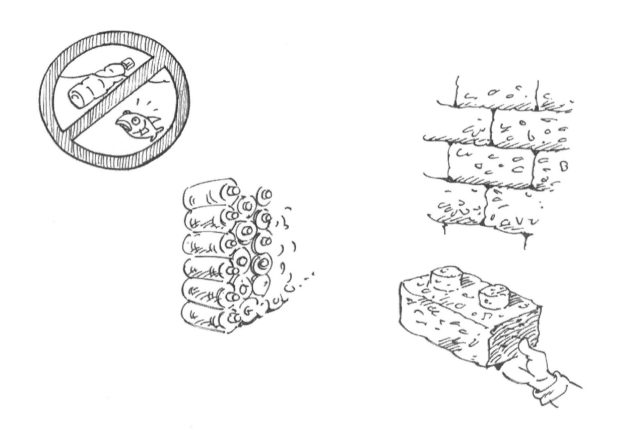

PLASTIC IS VERY HARD TO DESTROY, SO INSTEAD
OF THROWING IT IN THE OCEAN WHERE IT PERSISTS
ALMOST INDEFINITELY, MAKE IT INTO CHEAP,
LIGHT BRICKS WHERE ITS ENDURANCE IS USEFUL.
COLOMBIANS CONSTRUCT THEIR HOUSES FROM IT.

One of the doubtful qualities of plastic is the fact that it virtually indestructible, although it fragments into smaller and smaller pieces and enters the food chain where it does no good either. If we continue as we are doing, we will turn our oceans into waste-dumps and cease to derive edible fish from it. The plastic will end up in our own bodies, unless we eschew fish. This bodes ill for the environment and for human health, not to mention the plastics industry. But plastic remains very useful in its right place. Where is this? Its right place is where proving indestructible is a virtue, to wit, building materials. It is possible to make plastic into bricks by collecting the waste and not letting it enter rivers, seas and oceans. These take myriad forms, three of which are illustrated opposite. Bricks can be made from plastic bottles joined by mortar. The air and space inside the bottles is a good insulator from hot and cold climates, in much the same way as a string vest keeps the body warm by pockets of air. Such a wall is not transparent but it is translucent and walls can provide illumination. Bricks made from plastic are very light, cheap and easy to handle. In Colombia do-it-yourself houses have been constructed for as little as $5,500 from plastic waste which would otherwise end up in land-fill. Since bricks are made in moulds, it is possible to construct them like LEGO bricks so they can be joined together. If no longer viable, bricks of plastic are easy to disassemble and recycle. The plastics industry needs to be nimble and on its toes. In every crisis there is an opportunity, as the Chinese like to say.

Following best-practice in financing

"When she finally receives her loan, she is literally trembling and shaking. The money is burning her fingers. Tears roll down from her eyes, because she has never seen so much money in her life. She never imagined it in her hand. She carries it like a delicate bird or rabbit... until someone tells her to put it away in a safe place. For the first time in her life, an institution has trusted her...She is stunned, she will struggle to see every penny is paid back, and it is."
Muhammad Yunus

Lend to mothers and the money goes into the bodies and brains of their children. Of course, she repays. The alternative is to watch her children sicken and die and she has five other women backing her up.

Micro-financing as described and practiced by Mohammad Yunus and the Grameen bank in Bangladesh is a brilliant example to the world. Never was a Nobel Prize for Peace better deserved. Taken as a whole, micro-financing world-wide has had a patchwork of success and failures but this is because we did not look at what Yunus achieved with sufficient understanding. We believe the lessons are as follows. To be poor is to be unable to give to others or even reciprocate when others help you. It breaks the spirit to be always on the receiving end and compete at relative wretchedness. Repayment of the loan turns you from a beggar and object of charity to an independent business woman supporting your family, an entrepreneur, far more numerous in emerging economies. Lending to mothers and the empowerment of women are other keys, because the money lent will go straight to the bodies and brains of children and the supplies needed for her to work and keep them nourished. The alternative is to watch helpless while they starve. It is an important condition of loans that the children must be in full-time education, the roof in good repair and the earth toilet at least ten feet from house. Grameen had a 97.5% repayment rate which is the envy of many conventional banks and much, much higher than Bangladeshi banks generally. It made profits for every one of the 21 years Yunus was in charge of it and paid dividends to its owner-customers. It awarded scholarships to the children of customers, took beggars off the streets and supplied mobile phones at low cost. While it took money from foundations in its early years, it was entirely self-sufficient at its prime. It was resolutely non-bureaucratic with few, if any, paper records. Each borrower has five other women vouching for her who become eligible for loans if she repays. In practice they will pool resources rather than default, In the picture opposite the mother has bought a pedal powered sewing machine for $50 and is ten times more productive than before. She is no longer at the mercy of middle-men and loan sharks. The poor, if given half a chance, are amazingly resourceful to have survived at all. As C.K. Prahalad put it, there is "a fortune at the bottom of the pyramid", provided that you first care.

INVESTING IN SOCIALLY SIGNIFICANT INNOVATION

WE MUST PAY MORE ATTENTION TO VALUES WITHOUT SUBSTANCE

Triodus Bank, headed by Peter Blom in the Netherlands, was conceived as an idea during the Paris student revolt but did not finally take shape until the late 80s. It does not speculate with its money via mainstream banks, and only lends to business which it regards as benefitting the wider society. A bank must be dedicated to enterprising clients rather than itself, and only profit from their dedication and ensuing success. It has never made a loss in its whole history. Those depositing money with the bank are entitled to know about the good projects to which their money is being put, be it organic agriculture, art for the public, microloans for minorities or products protecting the environment; information will be supplied on request. Although it has branches in the Netherlands, Belgium, the UK and Spain, it does not intend to grow beyond medium size. Banks should serve local needs and relate intimately to their clients. This is best done by small independent units.

Peter Blom helped to found GABV, the Global Alliance for Banking on Values, which now has 50 members in more than 30 countries, who subscribe to its values and is growing at around 60% a year. He believes that the network should be large (and cooperative), not its units. The network assessed its own effectiveness with the help of a grant from a foundation. It was not only more profitable than the world's 25 largest banks but safer and less volatile. It famously grew 30% during 2008, the worst year ever for conventional banks. The slogan about 'following your heart but using your head' is vital to understanding its appeal. Clients are happy that the money they are depositing helps improve societies but they expect a first-rate banking service which is prudent with their money. You do NOT expect to be worse off for helping other people. You expect to gain.

COULD THE GAMBLING INDUSTRY HELP BUSINESS START-UPS?

ONE IN FIVE START-UPS DO NOT MAKE IT. THIS IS ENOUGH TO DETER EVEN A VENTURE CAPITALIST AND A BANK WOULD AVERT ITS GAZE, BUT FOR THE GAMBLING FRATERNITY THESE ARE ATTRACTIVE ODDS. MOREOVER, MOST GAMBLERS WOULD WIN ON AVERAGE AND RECEIVE MUCH MORE THAN FOUR TIMES THEIR STAKE IF THE COMPANY TOOK OFF.

The odds against any new business start-up succeeding is about 1 in 5. This does not tempt the stock-market at all and even Angel investors and Venture capitalists need to be smart enough to greatly reduce these odds against failing. However, one chance in five is equivalent to a bookmaker's odds of 4-1 against, a most attractive price for many gamblers, somewhere between favouritism and second favouritism in a typical horse-race. There are millions of people who gladly accept such odds. Americans are estimated to have lost $119 billion gambling in 2017. British gamblers lost $19.6 billion and Germans – one of the lowest in Europe - $14.6 billion. As much as a third of all stakes stay with the gambling industry and are not returned to winning punters. Why do people bet in this way? In part they do it because the process is rewarding. They are in effect "buying excitement". The occasional win stays in their minds much longer than the usual loss and they relive moments of triumph and celebration. For many it represents the only chance in their lives for abnormally high returns and the sole opportunity for upward mobility. Were sections of the gambling industry to invite wagers on start-ups whose chances of making it were 4-1 or worse, this form of gambling would represent a positive net return for punters. Instead of losing billions of dollars, they would make billions. Even a product at 4-1 against might actually pay 100-1 if it took off and flourished. Moreover, ventures would be launched much earlier before VCs or Angels were prepared to risk their cash. Also, failure can be a valuable lesson; the earlier you attempt something the sooner you improve your aim and try again. We should be trying new things even where the odds are against us. As of now, the gambling industry destroys wealth. Money simply moves from exploited to exploiters, at the end of which there is less to go around. How different it could be! We could have betting shops in the UK selling shares in start-up companies and producing returns that make all other betting a game for mugs. Wagering would actually pay most people.

❧

THE WELFARE CONSORTIUM:
HELPING THE POOR TO ORGANIZE

THOSE ON WELFARE COULD SAVE US BILLIONS IF THEY WERE ALLOWED TO ORGANIZE AND LAUNCH SOCIAL ENTERPRISES. HUGE AMOUNTS OF WORK NEEDS TO BE DONE AND A SENSE OF COMMUNITY RESTORED.

When Gerald Ford was running for re-election as President, the British author was informally approached by someone from SRI International at Menlo Park. Would I be interested in exploring the idea of welfare consortia as instruments to combat poverty? I was interested and still am. Ford lost to Carter and the idea died. We seek to re-awaken it. If 100 people receiving $25,000 a year were to pool their entitlements, they would have $2.5 million between them. Think what you could do with that! They might even give back 10% to begin with, so much would they save on bulk purchase, healthy food, shared possessions, lower energy use. The poor must organize to serve their communities. To be poor is to have nothing to give, but consortia of up to 125 members, (more than that and you cannot retain intimate relations), would all volunteer to work. Even old ladies would bake cakes. They would be dedicated to repaying their communities for what they received by serving that community in ways illustrated opposite. They would do this work for nothing unless recipients chose to give gratuities as some would. The huge advantage to getting paid for nothing specific, is to try something new and experimental in exchange. Consortia would be headed by a middle-class social entrepreneur. Members could give eight weeks of free labour to new ventures, after which they must be paid by that burgeoning enterprise, if it takes off. For example, insulating social housing for free could be paid for by subsequent reductions in energy bills. All consortia must get 20% of their members into paid work each year and take on new recipients. Consortia are launching pads for ideas to sustain communities. They do essential unpriced work. Would it work? It could hardly be worse than the present practice of paying people to do nothing and regarding every initiative at self-help as an attempt to cheat the welfare system! Even live-in lovers can deprive you of welfare. It needs you to be alone or dependent. Our competitors in East Asia look after their families and communities and spend far less on welfare. It will break us if unreformed.

⦿

F). MOVING FROM THINKING TO DOING

OVERCOMING THE CRISIS OF PURPOSE IN CONTEMPORARY CAPITALISM:
DEVELOPING ALL STAKEHOLDERS AND THEIR SKILLS

THE BIG INNOVATION CENTRE HAS PLEDGED TO
BE A CATALYST FOR CHANGE IN BRITISH SOCIETY.
AMONG ITS RECOMMENDATIONS ARE A SOVEREIGN
WEALTH FUND, A NEW COMPANIES ACT WHICH
SUPPORTS THOSE INVESTING LONG TERM...

Will Hutton, with the Purposeful Company taskforce of the Big Innovation Centre, sees the only solution to the woes of Western capitalism in what the task force calls "a crisis of purpose". This may be intangible but it holds us together. Capitalism is the only game in town but it must empower all its stakeholders, employees, unions, consumers and suppliers especially. No one owns our public corporations and banks any more, save traders shuffling paper shares, demanding instant gains in their value with scant regard for the future of the actual enterprise. We extract money from corporations, which we then throw away, together with their people, their spirits and their values, instead of investing in the future growth and innovation of enterprise. Britain's productivity is abysmal, now 16% below the trend line and among the worst in Europe. The UK has an unequal reward system constituting a Frankenstein monster. The industrial giants of the Thirties are gone and foreign nations like TATA and BMW are busy buying up what remains. One third of listed companies have disappeared in the last decade. The 8% of the UK's children educated in private schools have huge advantages, like 70% of the judiciary. No wonder public education is a step-child and the smart society stymied.

Hutton co-chairs the Purposeful Company task-force of the Big Innovation Centre, an award-winning "do tank" and innovation hub led by CEO Birgitte Andersen, which has pledged to be a catalyst for change in British society. Among its recommendations are: a sovereign wealth fund should replace the toothless Shareholder Executive; the end of debt as a tax-reducing device; a new Companies Act supporting those who invest long-term by increasing the voting power of those shares while depriving short-term speculators of voting rights; no rights at all for anonymous owners; no capital gains on shares held briefly; and classes of shares reflecting commitment to a company as American Unicorn companies do already. Not-for-profit mutual companies would gather proxy votes to be exercised on behalf of stewardship of the environment and the development of human beings at work. Make it much harder to take over well-managed companies like Cadbury, require employees to be consulted, require a two-thirds majority if the defending board objects to the bid and bar from voting all those merely speculating on the outcome. Mutually owned assets must stay mutually owned and publicly benefit companies launched to show these are more, not less profitable in the end.

THE GOD THAT LIMPS

IT IS SOCIO-TECHNICAL SYSTEMS THAT IMPROVE/CRIPPLE OUR WORLD

In the entire Greek Pantheon there was only one imperfect god, Hephaestus, blacksmith to the gods who limped as he walked. He was part-object. Limping was a metaphor for errors in judgement. Oedipus limped, (the name means "swollen foot"), as did his father and grandfather. There are social systems and technical systems merging together to form a socio-technical system, common in most businesses. We use various production techniques, but these alter the social systems charged with operating them. It is commonly thought that techniques are neutral and if they are destructive, this is because their operators are. This is patent nonsense. If two persons in conflict are both armed, the biggest bigot will pull the trigger or stab first and the more responsible of the two will die. What technology does is to greatly increase certain key human capacities, like the ability to kill quickly. For every new and "better" way of doing things the social system is altered in some way and is frequently suffers unanticipated consequences. We often call such innovations "disruptive", claiming that they are the price of progress and that anyone demurring is a Luddite. As of now the USA is both the main source of innovative technologies and the nation most plagued with social problems. It limps along, dragging social crises in its wake.

One of the problems is the Two Cultures, the sciences and the humanities. Scientists may lack humanity and vice versa. Consider Uber, the ride-hailing technology; it is clearly more economic and more flexible than a taxi rank, but it also encourages casual labour and cheap part-time employment rather than professionalism among drivers. Like Facebook it charges madly ahead to dominate its market. Yet this argy-bargy is totally unnecessary. It would be easy to make drivers experts on most good restaurants in town, provide menus in the cab, book a table for you and drive you to your rendezvous. Drivers could specialize in all the town's museums, offer reviews of films and plays, advise on children's amusement and arrange trips on rivers and canals. The expertise needed of the driver could be specified in advance. Must we allow Facebook to sell our personality profiles, feature guides to self-harming, spread lies and hate, and locate opioid suppliers. Time was when those with fantasies of rape and torture would find it almost impossible to recruit fellow enthusiasts and gave up rather than appal friends; but various platforms make this easy. The foulest of fantasies can be secretly indulged and encouraged

Moreover, many technologies and forms of artificial intelligence confer great social benefits. Blockchains facilitate knowledge sharing and trust, see Birgitte Anderson on page 276. Cars that will not start until the seat-belt is fastened induce habits of a life-time, the humble stop-light is a brilliant lesson in take-your-turn. The god does not need to limp if we use social and emotional intelligence in its design. Alibaba has single-mindedly boosted the Chinese middle-class consumer for whom Communism never had much time. It lends its name and power to thousands of start-ups and guarantees deliveries and payments. Every form of AI must be looked at critically for the good or harm it bestows. We should have on-line platforms pledged to improve creative notions, without attacking the creators themselves. We need them to keep trying and finally taste the thrilling contrast between improving our society and communication or failing to do this.

Investing in Socially Significant Innovation
Innovative Technologies and the Big Innovation Centre

We must pay more attention to values without substance

The Big Innovation Centre is located a stone's throw from the Houses of Parliament and counts MPs and Lords from all political parties among its co-creators of innovative strategies to be deployed by the UK as a whole. These are what used to be called "the great and the good" (before Brexit) but are arguably central to national strategies. Professor Birgitte Andersen, a Danish national, who is Professor of Economics at Birkbeck College, the University of London, is the CEO of the Centre, which has enlisted private corporations, members of both Houses and sundry experts in the All-Party Parliamentary Group. Other initiatives include the Bank of England and the Intellectual Property Office. Her major focus is on the Intangible Economy of industrial eco-systems, quality, intellectual property and social purpose, all of which give an economy meaning and which drive its innovation. Research that BIC has conducted shows the UK lagging in tangibles like manufacturing but growing in intangibles. But these, like the bubbles in the picture opposite, are much harder to measure and to estimate and may burst on being touched. Banks often refuse to lend on intangible properties, a situation Andersen seeks to change. Companies need to report on their intangibles if they are to be adequately funded and valued. What distinguishes Andersen's approach is that she does not regard innovations as "technology free". Every industrial revolution has its key technologies, from the locomotive to the automobile to microchips and electronics. She has chosen Artificial Intelligence (AI) and the Blockchain as seminal technologies of the present age and takes her "stand" on these platforms (see picture). Just as many new companies use the Internet as a platform, so will many future companies mount themselves on the technologies illustrated. We must grasp that AI helps us to learn and that the challenge of the future is Learning to Learn, a process that reconciles hard skills like the algorithms in AI, with the soft skills of criticising, improving and inventing these initially. This is convincingly argued by Niki Iliadis, the Policy Foresight Manager at the Centre. AI and Blockchain must be our servants, not our masters. The Centre has won the Public Affairs Award for the Think Tank of 2018 and is working on property rights strategies.

Exhibition of the Future: Digital Prototypes Display New Products

We could protect our intellectual property rights by animating these on digital media and holding exhibitions, open to the world. This would give them substance and description and spur customers to try them.

I t is important as Professor Andersen has shown, to render what is insubstantial in a way that gives it substance. We saw earlier that to improve the prototype of your new product is to make this more elaborate, detailed, flexible and dramatic, so that more investors, employees, customers and partners are attracted, as the more imaginative your product becomes. The cost of digital recording has been dropping for years and if you want your new enterprise to be taken seriously then producing a cheap prototype not just of the product itself, but of its impact on the social and physical environment and what its customers can expect to do with it, becomes imperative. The actual hand-made prototype may be expensive while a filmed model of its operations might be much cheaper and relatively inexpensive for potential customers to modify so that you essentially co-create. Both Britain and the USA are among leaders in theatre, TV and movies. They are among the world's best entertainers, so they are in a very strong position in filming their own visions of the future and attracting a wide audience for innovation in general. The ideal is to get cultures enthralled. Exhibitions of the Future could be held in various countries with entries from the whole world. DVDs are used to put over the sometimes complex way in which antibodies protect our immune systems, how monitoring our vital functions can prolong your life, objects can be delivered by drones, and doctors' waiting rooms have a machine on which you register your symptoms and get a read-out which you hand to the doctor while consulting him/her. This is much quicker and raises possibilities the doctor might have missed. Showing a film of your ongoing project helps to establish your intellectual property should others try to steal it. Knowing what graphene can do makes all kinds of products possible. The objective is to get citizens rooting for a more creative culture with the media extolling this. Newspapers and TV which mobilize investors could charge commissions which helps to fund good journalism.

❧

BLOCK-CHAIN AS DISTRIBUTED TRUTH

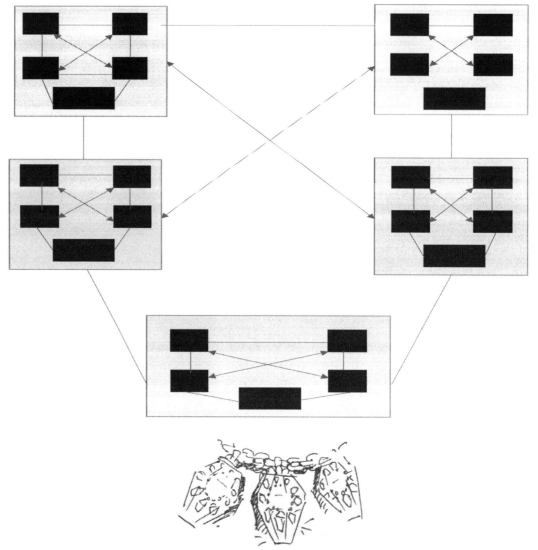

IN EVERY MACROCOSM A MICROCOSM,
LIKE THE DIAMOND SUTRA

What is a Blockchain? It is essentially a digital distributed ledger in which nodes (users) record and approve transactions. The updated ledger is distributed among all stakeholders in the network. The ledger keeps an immutable record of the transactions in the network. It could record many of the ideas suggested in this book. In some respects, it resembles the legendary diamond sutra, the book cites a bracelet in which every stone reflects on its surface the entire bracelet so that in every part there is a whole and in every whole there are parts. This concept was taught to Pericles by his tutor Anaxagoras in Ancient Athens. Within any functioning democracy there would be thousands of "democratic" human relationships in which people listened carefully and treated one another with respect, ensuring that even a minority got a hearing. In this book we have looked at fractals in nature. The tiny trees that are engraved on every leaf of that tree. The word fractal means "the same from near as from far." From far you see the whole, from near you see the parts, but these parts are reflections of the living whole. Creating wealth is a pattern which Blockchains could register.

You can put a spear through the back of someone's head so they lose a part of the striate cortex which records our memories. Curiously, no memories are lost and until recently we did not know why. But now we know that memory in the form of imagery is DISTRIBUTED, which means that like ripples on a pond, it records symmetrical-wave forms. Any small section of that wave-form records the whole. These ripples in the form of brain-waves remember the shape of the stone dropped into the "water". This book has likened value creation to wave-forms rather than rocks of righteousness.

One of the oldest lies we keep repeating is that technologies are neutral and rely entirely on the character and morality of the person using them. On the contrary, technologies like H-bombs facilitate the destruction of civilization, not its flowering. A knife or gun makes their use more likely and this is largely intimidating and destructive. We believe that Blockchain has built-in potential to enhance certain values in preference to others and if fully exploited could transform our societies. For example, a Blockchain has the potential to validate news and consensus around that truth rather than fake news. When a new transaction is entered into the ledger and agreed among peers a new version of the ledger is distributed between network integrands making it tamperproof. No one has the jump on anyone else. No one acts without others knowing this. It is transparent and evokes trust with a pool of distributed information and invites stakeholders to believe in each other. It records the fairness of relationships the prevalence of win-win and rids trade of costly intermediaries. It reveals injustices to wide audiences.

It favours equality and reduces hierarchy because everyone has the same knowledge at the same time, and it becomes impossible to deceive or withhold information. It decentralizes, distributes and empowers diverse people rather than social distance becoming an invitation to deceive and exploit. The implementation of Blockchain technology in the supply-chain could assure you the provenance of diamonds purchased and whether this was violent, what everyone in the supply chain has contributed and received in exchange, especially miners (who also have access to this information). If you wished as a customer to know, it could record salary differentials, late payments to suppliers, the bankruptcy occasioned by such forced loans, gender inequality, zero-hour contracts, the amount spent on training and R&D, complaints by employees and customers, the taxes paid by a company, reductions in carbon emissions, the use of renewable energy, the elimination of toxins, ratings by consumer organizations, & fines levied by regulators. It could arm and empower consumers with detailed knowledge of the good and harm done by a company, who could adjust their purchases.

Notes on Part V

1 Figure Ground relationships

Our position is that vice and virtue are descriptively different in their structure and it is not difficult to tell them apart. Contrasting values are either harmonized (virtue) or split apart (vice). The major influence on us is Gregory Bateson see *Steps to an Ecology of Mind* , New York, Ballantine 1972..

2 True virtue lies in reconciled opposites: Vice is disorder.

See *Nine Visions of Capitalism,* Charles Hampden-Turner and Fons Trompenaars, Oxford: Infinite Ideas Press 2015

3 Skills, challenges and values that fuse and transcend.

See Mihaly Csikszentmihalyi *Flow: The Psychology of Optimal Experience* New York, Harper, 1990, a highly successful study of happiness.

4 Values and Meta-Values: Liberty and Fraternity weighed Equally

We read of this in *The Age of Paradox* by Charles Handy, Boston: Harvard Business School Press, 1988. This was entitled *The Empty Raincoat* in the UK.

5 Values as upward spirals and spinning Frisbees 1

I was convinced of this by Theo Kroese in the Netherlands and we attempted a book proposal without success.

6 Values as upward spirals and spinning Frisbees 2

The rotation of the Frisbee is what keeps it flying straight. It is similar with values.

7 Diversity of values and their relative merit

For the whole notion of "heterarchy", I am in debt to Jay Ogilvy, see *Many Dimensional Man*, Oxford University Press, 1977. It was Jean Paul Sartre who pointed out that we admire a blind pianist because he is blind. We can praise him without the least reduction in our own relative standing among sighted people since he differs so much from us. When the British author taught entrepreneurship to classes in Singapore, the level of mutual support was amazing. Their projects were so different as to be incomparable. We can be best-in-class where classes differ. The success of any one project did not diminish the others. Difference is a many splendored phenomenon.

8 Universalism taken too far: Laws squeezing out relationships

The joke was related to us by Henry Mintzberg but is common currency in North America.

9 Contracts taken too far: Relationships of mutuality

The story is told by Charles Handy in *The Age of Paradox* op. cit.

10 Individualism taken too far: The Social Purpose is lost

This picture is drawn from a mimeo draft given to us by Henry Mintzberg.

11 Atomism/analysis taken too far: whole meanings lost.

A poet like W.H. Auden joins things together. Are we in danger of reducing reality to meaningless rubble?

12 Values as waves with frequency and amplitude

See Elliott Jaques *The Form of Time,* New York: Crane Russak,1982. How quickly one value follows upon its contrast is an insight largely lost to the world but of huge import.

13. The Traffic Light as a benign rotation

Edmund Leach, Levi-Strauss. Fontana Moderns Masters, 1982 London, 1981. Levi-Strauss was known to be dissatisfied by this version of his life's work.

14 Values are reconciled in synergy or split apart.

The official name for values coming apart is "schismogenesis...the growing split in the structure of values and ideas", coined by Gregory Bateson in *Steps to an Ecology of Mind* op. cit. pp.60-72. It has yet to make it into the dictionary. He first penned it as the Nazi menace was growing in Germany, but too few read it. Churchill recognized the pattern, "the Nazi is either at your knees or at your throat," but we have still to identify and warn against its recognizable form. The present wave of populism shows it has not left us!

15 THE INTEGRATED VALUES OF DEMOCRACY

See Paul Watzlawick, *How Real is Real*, New York Vintage 1977.

16 SOFT VALUES CAN PROVOKE HARD VALUES: TRAGEDY MAY RESULT

See Gregory Bateson "Culture Contact and Schismogenesis" in *Steps to an Ecology of Mind* op.cit. pp 60-72. The love shown by Billy Budd to the Master at Arms in Melville's novel shows that even love, loyalty and innocence can provoke their opposites and lead to judicial murder.

17 RECONCILING SELF AND OTHER, EGOISM AND ALTRUISM

All this was pointed out by Ruth Benedict in *Patterns of Culture*. New York: Houghton-Mifflin, 1989. She found that societies were happy where altruistic acts were promptly repaid, hence restoring the self-interest of those deeply concerned for others. She called this Synergy, an idea taken up and championed by Abraham Maslow, see *Motivation and Personality* New York: Harper and Row, 1954

18 COURAGE AND CAUTION: RECONCILED

It was Pericles in his famous funeral oration who said that fallen Athenians – but perhaps not the Spartans they fought against -- knew the sweetness and beauties of life but were still prepared to risk their precious lives. A suicide bomber is reckless and fails to value life – his own or others.

19 OBEDIENCE AND HARMONY: DISOBEDIENCE AND DISRUPTION

Clayton Christensen has made disruption part of industrial practice, see *The Innovator's Dilemma* Boston: Harvard Business School Press, 1997. Apple 1 was able to put most of the functions of a mainframe computer into a PC and disrupt it.

20 STEADFAST LOYALTY AND PRINCIPLED DISSENT

E.M. Forster said that given a choice of betraying his friends or his country, he hoped to find the courage to betray the latter. This makes sense, because the country is an extension of those you know and love within that country and if you betray them, you sacrifice humanity for an abstraction.

21 SOLITARY APPEAL TO SOLIDARITY: THE METOO MOVEMENT

Much here depends on timing. We only realized Socrates was right after Plato wrote him up. He had to die first. The first women to protest against sexual harassment by men are typically ignored or paid off. But after so many complainants are rebuffed, a woman puts a match to a critical mass of indignation and the whole scandal catches fire.

22 CRITICISING AND SUPPORTING EMPLOYEES

Note that giving or withholding a bonus completely kills this message. Money is a very crude way of judging.

23 COACHING FOR DIVERSITY AND INCLUSION

Identity politics which has occasioned much comment of late, is a claim to be included not for what you have done or communicated but for what you are, a white male, an evangelical, a transgender person or a bisexual. Such identities may not be challenged and speakers doing this are denied a hearing on campus.

24 WORLD VALUES ARE MIRROR IMAGES OF ONE ANOTHER 1

See *Riding the Waves of Culture* Fons Trompenaars and Charles Hampden-Turner, London Nicholas Brealey, 2013, (3rd Edition).

Gregory Bateson used to ask why Satan was left-handed; because he is the backward reflection of ourselves.

25 WORLD VALUES ARE MIRROR IMAGES OF ONE ANOTHER 2

This brings us considerable closer but still convinced that the other is "subverting" us by touting the value we have neglected. If communism is a foul conspiracy, then this not only allows Americans to deny that they lack a community ethic, it encourages them to close ranks against the enemy and so emulate his solidarity!

26 DEVELOPING VALUES AT HIGHER LEVELS OF INTEGRATION

An interesting argument has arisen as to whether an intellectual scaffolding for moral decisions is needed. A number of female heroines have been interviewed who clearly exemplified level 6 but could give no intellectual defence. "He would have died unless I helped him" was a typical rejoinder. It seems we can act intuitively without explaining it to ourselves or others.

27 SUCCESSIVE STAGES OF INTER-CULTURAL SENSITIVITY

Learning about others is indivisible from learning more about ourselves. Between us we share the human condition and the stranger may know about our estranged values.

28 Trompenaars' first two dimensions

All this is laid out in Fons Trompenaars and Charles Hampden-Turner *Riding the Waves of Culture,* op cit. For illustrations see Charles Hampden-Turner and Fons Trompenaars *Building Cross-Cultural Competence,* Chichester, John Wiley, 2000. The finding that Western women managers have values closer to those of East Asia is a good argument for empowering women to the point of equality

29 A second pair of dimensions by Trompenaars & Berlin

See *Riding the Waves of Culture* op. cit. Note that diffuse and cooperative viewpoints that exclude the specifics and individuals may tend to totalitarianism. However, it is easier for the whole to include the parts than the parts the whole. Relationships between the two may be the key to creating wealth.

30 Trompenaars's last two dimensions

Inner direction is very much involved in US gun culture. At the pull of a trigger you can negate twenty years of nurture with those who are the most bigoted shooting first and winning. At its source is distrust of government authority. Once again, women managers seem to have the values missing in the West. Giving them greater influence may be the quickest way to turning Western economies around.

Notes for Part VI

31 Combining Opposed Values

Basic Value Template. See Charles Hampden-Turner, *Charting the Corporate Mind* Oxford: Basil Blackwell, 1994

32 Teams and Relationships; Hawthorne and the Informal System.

Fritz Roethlisberger and William Dickson, *Management and the Worker* Cambridge MA. Harvard University Press, 1939. Our interpretation is in Chapter 8 of Charles Hampden-Turner's *Radical Man* New York: Doubleday Anchor, 1982

33 The Managerial Grid: Fusing People with Tasks, Arts with Science

See Robert Blake and Jane S Mouton, *Managing Intergroup Conflict in Industry* Houston: Gulf Publishing, 1965

34 Teams tend to develop over time

See "Stages of Small Group Development Revisited" by Bruce Tuckman and Mary Ann C Jensen *Group and Organizational Studies.* volume 2 no.4 1977 pp.419-27

35 Self-fulfilling prophecies — the importance of Theory Y

See Douglas McGregor *The Human Side of the Enterprise* New York: McGraw Hill, 1960. America has long benefitted from its all-purpose optimism about business and people and its habit of treating strangers as equals. However, there is no substitute for actually knowing the particular person. Generalized bonhomie has its limitations.

36. The Process of Continuous Improvement

W. Edwards Deming *Out of the Crisis*: Cambridge MA. MIT Press. For gain-sharing and fate-sharing see Edward E.Lawler III's *High Involvement Management* San Francisco, Jossey-Bass, 1986

37. High Context is a measure of rich relationships.

Royal Foote "Wright Institute working paper": mimeo, Wright Institute, Berkeley, Ca. 1978

38 Low-cost, high quantity products vs. high quality premium products

For this underlying distinction in all business strategies see Michael E. Porter *Competitive Strategy,* New York: Free Press, 1980. He has long insisted that the two appeals do not mix, save to weaken each other. We do not agree. Behind every high quantity low cost product, is a quality, sometimes taken for granted. Buying cheaper eggs one in ten of which are bad would not work.

39 A high-quality competent builder or a cut-price cowboy?

Fons Trompenaars knows John Cleese and has appeared on platforms with him.

40 Lexus: Low-cost fused with premium quality

The volume car makers have generally got the best of those who specialize in high-price premium products on their own like Rolls Royce.

41. Dell Computers with a strategic and customised purpose.

A combination of very cheap parts and customized software seems to have done the trick.

42 Socio-technical learning as the key to development

In addition to D A Kolb et al *Organizational Psychology,* Englewood Cliffs, NJ: Prentice-Hall, 1974 see also Eric Trist and K Bamforth "Some social and psychological consequences of the long-wall method of coal getting" in *Human Relations 4* pp.3-38

43. Reconciling Abstract-Concrete, Active-Reflective

Rejoicing in the fact that new technologies "disrupt", prevents us from choosing technologies which are socially more positive. Does our social system need to dragged behind technological change? Should we not be the masters of our tools rather than their slaves?

44. Change and Continuity

Gary Hamel in "Strategic Intent" in the *Harvard Business Review* May-June 1989 argues that you can maintain and build on your core competence, fusing change with continuity.

45. Change, continuity and corner stoning

This concept comes from Adrian Slywotsky and Richard Wise, *How to Grow when Markets Don't* New York, Warner Business Books 2003

46 CHANGE WORKS BEST WITH CONTINUITY OF DIRECTION.

C H-T used to teach innovation at Nanyang Technological University in Singapore and my classes were taken to Orchidville in its various stages. We saw it unfold.

47. COMPETE AT COOPERATING: THE ART OF CO-OPETITION

See Adam Brandenburger and Barry J. Nalebuff *Co-opetition* New York: Currency, Doubleday, 1996

48 HOW COMPETITION AT IBM HELPED TO SPUR COOPERATION

This account was given to C H-T personally by Tim Gallwey.

49. COMPETING AT TOTAL CUSTOMER SATISFACTION AT MOTOROLA

This situation was one to which C H-T consulted in 1988

50 HOW MACHO TRUCK DRIVERS BECAME KNIGHTS OF THE ROAD

This was related to C H-T by colleagues at The Wright Institute, Berkeley California. circa 1980. He was told that the name of the oil company could not be divulged.

51 RULES VS. EXCEPTIONS: AUSTRALIA VS. JAPAN

See Charles Hampden-Turner and Fons Trompenaars, *The Seven Cultures of Capitalism*: London, Piatkus, 1992   Chapter 2

52. Samsung as an exception to the rule. Was our copyright infringed?

This is a true story and happened to Fons Trompenaars. See *Riding the Waves of Cultures* op cit.

53. Southwest Airlines: rules, exceptions and humour

In humour lies the recognition that values clash unexpectedly. Southwest and its culture has a fascinating resemblance to what Tom Peters and Bob Waterman wrote in *In Search of Excellence* New York: Simon and Schuster, 1982

54. The Two Gods of Time: Chronos and Kairos

See Elliott Jaques *The Form of Time* op.cit.

55. Time and Motion (America) vs. Just in Time (Japanese)

Charles Hampden-Turner and Fons Trompenaars *Building Cross-Cultural Competence.* Chichester: John Wiley, 2000 pp.320-328

56. Teams solving problems over time

GE's work-out groups are famous. There are descriptions on the Internet

57 Can a confident leader be a humble servant?

See Fons Trompenaars and Ed Voerman, *Servant Leadership Across Cultures* Oxford: Infinite Ideas Press. 2009

58. How humble service can elevate you to the top.

100 Plus Management Models by Fons Trompenaars and Piet Hein Coebergh Oxford: Infinite Ideas Press, 2014 p.426

59. A triumph of Self-effacement: Wretched bureaucrat learns to live.

Ikiru (To live) 1952 Japan black and white film, director Akira Kurosawa. Donald Richie The Films of Akira Kurosawa Berkeley: University of California Press, 1984

60. Serving the Infinite Game, not the Finite Game

James P. Carse, *Finite and Infinite Games.* New York: Ballantine, 1986

63. Understanding that Wholes are more than Parts

Stephen Nachmanovitch's doctoral dissertation on William Blake's 'Maps of the Deep' at UC Santa Cruz, 1971

64. Parts and Wholes: How IKEA does it.

Charles Hampden-Turner and Fons Trompenaaars *Building Cross-Cultural Competence* op.cit.

65 Knowledge is whole. Data are but parts.

Fons Trompenaars and Charles Hampden-Turner *Managing People Across Cultures* Chichester, Capstone, 2004 p.173

66 CREATING WHOLES OUT OF CHEAP STANDARDIZED MODULES.

See note 64

67. THE FIVE STAGES OF EVOLUTION

None of the stages are wrong, but nor are they sufficient in themselves and where they are exaggerated, they become dysfunctional. The idea that a single genius builds a company, completely overlooks the help received, sheer good fortune, favourable circumstances and the loyal service of dedicated agents. The notion that there are scientific laws for corporate excellence that cause things to work with machine-like precision overlooks personal judgment and pre-selects what is predictable. Business schools serve large, mature organizations and very few MBAs become entrepreneurs. Indeed, most of industry cannot afford MBAs from good schools. They go into finance or consulting. That human relationships are key, tends to get overlooked because these are immeasurable and no one party is "in control". Where science resembles physics, there is 'I-it' rather than 'I-Thou' connections. It is mutuality that creates wealth, not manipulation. We think shareholders should get better returns, but where they short-change other stakeholders they harm themselves. Sustainability is a worthy goal and saving the planet is more inspiring than just manufacturing carpets but unless you do this profitably you cannot long survive. Most important of all is to get the five stages in an optimal relationship and in a virtuous circle spirally upwards.

Notes for Part VII

67 CREATIVITY AND INNOVATION: A RECOURSE FOR DEVELOPED NATIONS

Peter Drucker is among those who state that already affluent nations need to fill their products with knowledge and innovative acts, see Peter F. Drucker *Innovation and Entrepreneurship* New York: Routledge 2007.

68. ACTS OF CREATION

The Act of Creation by Arthur Koestler London: Hutchinson, 1964. Note that what is new is the association, not the parts associated.

69. FIERCE CONCENTRATION AND GENTLE RELAXATION

Teresa Amabile "Creativity under the Gun," *Harvard Business Review* August 2002

70. THE HARE AND THE TORTOISE - POUNCE AND PONDER

Guy Claxton *Hare Brain, Tortoise Mind.* London: Fourth Estate Ltd. 1987. When you have problem and sleep on it, the answer often pops into your head.

71 DIVERGING THE BETTER TO CONVERGE ON A SOLUTION

J. W. Getzels and P. W. Jackson *Creativity and Intelligence* New York: Wiley, 1962

72. Divergence and Convergence form a search pattern

Note that you must diverge first to discover the scent or the field of play. A psychoanalyst has his client free-associate.

73. Vertical and lateral thinking

Edward de Bono *Lateral Thinking* New York: Harper and Row, 1970

74. Golden Ages: The Rare Combination of Cash with Artistry

Being innovative tends to raise anxiety in a populace, engulfed in novelty. Michelangelo at one time threw his own pictures on the bonfire as he was denounced by Savonarola, the anti-Renaissance priest. Rollo May has pointed out that the pupils in the eyes of those Michelangelo and others painted dilated over time. This is a symptom of growing anxiety. The Medicis as bankers with violent histories were barely respectable in the eyes of many.

75. Playing precedes serious intentions

Michael Schrage *Serious Play* Boston: Harvard Business School Press, 1999

76. Thinking processes of highly creative architects.

Frank Barron in *Creativity and Personal Freedom* New York: Van Nostrand, 1968

77 Innovation requires a Critical environment

Managing People Across Cultures Fons Trompenaars and Charles Hampden-Turner, Chichester: Capstone, 2004 p. 152

78. INNOVATION NEEDS DIFFERENCES TO BE INTEGRATED

Paul R. Lawrence and Jay W. Lorsch *Organisation and Environment* Boston: Harvard Business School Division of Research, 1967

79. ERRING, CORRECTING AND CONTINUOUSLY IMPROVING I

W. Edwards Deming *Out of the Crisis* Cambridge: The MIT Press, 1982

80 ERRING, CORRECTING AND CONTINUOUSLY IMPROVING II

See previous note

81 INNOVATION MUST BE OPEN TO THE LARGER ECOSYSTEM

Henry Chesbrough *Open Services Innovation.* Boston: Harvard Business School Press, 2003. More and more are services bundled up with products so goods supplied are also installed, maintained and users trained. It may take several cooperating companies to do this.

82. IS INNOVATION INTERNAL TO A COMPANY OR EXTERNAL?

Charles Hampden-Turner and Fons Trompenaars *Building Cross-Cultural Competence* Chichester: John Wiley, 2000 p. 196

83. THE CAMBRIDGE PHENOMENON: THE ECONOMY OF THE FUTURE

C Hampden-Turner and Fons Trompenaars *Nine Visions of Capitalism*. Oxford: Infinite Ideas Press 2015, chapter 10

84. INNOVATION AND THE UNIVERSITY'S DIVERSITY OF KNOWLEDGE

Personal communication with Gordon Edge. See also note 75 on the importance of being able to 'play'. Universities offer a moratorium from busy work in which we can experiment and ruminate, both essential to the creative process.

85 THE SPIN-OFF AND THE PARENT-OFFSPRING RELATIONSHIP

Elizabeth Garnsey and Paul Heffernan "Clustering through spin-out and attraction", *Regional Studies* (39) 8th November 2005

86. THE WE COMPANY: DESIGNING A CULTURE OF INNOVATION

Personal communication with Gaia Trompenaars and Internet descriptions

Notes on Part VIII

87 Sustain what sustains us

William Blake brilliantly conveyed the paradoxical structure of nature I am indebted to Steven Nachmanovitch and his doctoral dissertation "Job's Return" at the University California 1976, Santa Cruz who explored Blake in depth.

88 Work with the earth's natural forces: The Triple Bottom Line

John Elkington *Cannibals with Forks: The Triple Bottom Line of 21st Business* Capstone, Oxford 1997

89 Ascending Mount Sustainability: Seven Steps

Ray C. Anderson *Business Lessons from a Radical Industrialist,* New York: St. Martin's Griffin, 2009

90 Profits from Saving the Environment

See previous note

91 Cradle to Cradle: Products which regenerate

William McDonough and Michael Braungart *Cradle to Cradle: Remaking the way we make things* New York: Northpoint Press, 2002 see also *The Upcycle: Beyond Sustainability-Designing for Abundance.* North Point Press, 2013 by the same authors.

92. The Greening of our Cities

See previous note

93 Harnessing the Sun and Wind to reach the Tipping Point

The Press reports that China leads the world in solar technology. Salesmen go from rural village to village with portable, solar heated showers in their vans or on their backs.

94 Industrial Symbiosis: relating waste to raw material

Kalundborg Symbiosis in Denmark is described on the Internet, see also Kalundborg Eco-Park.

95. Three New Alliances: 1. NGOs and for-profit companies

C.K. Prahalad's *The Fortune at the Bottom of the Pyramid*, Philadelphia: Wharton School Publishing, 2004 gives many examples of how businesses can help NGOs and the social goals of governments.

96. New Alliance: 2. Consumers with Best Practice companies.

IKEA's largely successful attempts to improve the environment by the way it purchases its inventories repays careful study.

97. Can profits fund progressive social policies? The case of Unilever.

Much of this is thanks to Paul Polman.

98. Might consumers be willing to buy social justice?

Ben and Jerry has pushed its highly humane agenda and this has certainly done it no harm. It was purchased by Unilever, who has allowed it to influence its human resource policies.

99 Can we buy a better world? The Character of the Corporation

C H-T first suggested this in 1974 during the American war on poverty, see *From Poverty to Dignity: Strategy for Poor Americans*. New York: Doubleday, 1974. No one took any notice at all. He still thinks it is a good idea!

100. New Alliances 3. Get the online community on our side

Charlene Li and Josh Bernoff *Groundswell: Winning in a World Transformed by Social Technologies.* Boston: Harvard Business School Press, 2011

101. The Changing Face of Marketing

C. Gronroos *Service Management and Marketing* Chichester: John Wiley, 2007

102. Only for-profit companies have the power to scale up

This is emphasised in Michael Porter's TED talk on the Internet.

103. Government as Referee, Commander or Coach

This issue was raised by Bruce Scott and George C Lodge in *US Competitiveness and the World Economy* Boston: Harvard Business School Press, 1985. The truth is that the USA and its government intervenes massively in its economy in the name of defence and always has since the outset of World War I. This is in effect, a subsidy to high tech.

104. Governing by Artful Nudges

Richard H Thaler and Cass R. Sunstein *Nudge: Improving Decisions About Health, Wealth and Happiness* London: Penguin Books, 2009

105 Was the Arms' Race the Secret of America's Economic Power?

Every new weapon lays the foundation and necessity for the next. We dare not fall behind in killing power however much this exceeds useful purposes. Sadly, many of these weapons would kill nearly everyone in the vicinity, if not the world. Killing is from so far away that we do not witness its cruelty and excess with our own eyes. So-called smart weapons cannot discriminate between a terrorist and the woman who does the laundry.

106. The role of the Federal Government in Apple's innovation

This argument is taken from Mariana Mazzucato *The Entrepreneurial State: Debunking Public vs. Private Sector Myths* London: Anthem Press, 2015

107 Are Microchips more valuable than potato chips?

Personal communication with Lester Thurow, see also *The Zero-sum Society* New York: McGraw Hill. 1980. To the extent that products include knowledge, they contribute to knowledge communities. Economics has been remarkably slow in seeing this.

108. What are the true value of infra-structure projects?

KPMG in the Netherlands is among the bodies preparing to measure this, see its study of the Dutch Railway system and what it contributes to the sustainability and effectiveness of the economy.

109 Values forming relationships of Synergy

Abraham Maslow, *Motivation and Personality* New York; Harper and Row, 1954

110 The Supreme human value emerging from this book is synergy

R Buckminster Fuller *Synergetics* London: Macmillan 1975

111 Values and Relationships - helping and healing

C Hampden-Turner *Sane Asylum* San Francisco Book Company, 1974 op cit

112 Paradoxes abound: The Dialectic Dance of Opposites

Linda Putman, see presentation at Nova University, Lisbon Leadership and Society Forum *"The Language of Paradox, Pluralism and Conflict"*, May 24th 2018

113 Dynamic Equilibrium

Wendy K Smith, Marianne Lewis and Michael Tushman, "Both/And Leadership" *Harvard Business Review,* May 2016

114 Leadership and the Experience of a Crucible in your past life

Warren Bennis, Daniel Goleman and James O'Toole, *Transparency: How Leaders Create a Culture of Candour.* San Francisco. Jossey-Bass, 2010

115. Alibaba: A platform company and social justice

Duncan Clark *Alibaba: The House That Jack Ma Built.* New York: Harper Collins, 2011

116 Kickstarter, the crowdfunder which recently became a B Corporation

Extensively described on the Internet.

117. Crowd-funding comes to Prime-time Television

C H T regards this as obvious and surely coming soon. Why do we not act now?

118 Plastic in the right place

Bricks made from recycled plastic are much featured on the Internet. We need the endurance of plastic where it is useful, not in the oceans.

119 FOLLOW BEST-PRACTICE IN FINANCING

Muhammad Yunus has clearly demonstrated that providing micro-loans to the poor requires that you CARE about them initially. The score of imitators have largely lost the plot, see *Banker to the Poor: The Story of Grameen Bank* London: Aurum Press, 2003.

120 FOLLOW YOUR HEART, USE YOUR HEAD

Peter Blom's feat in founding GABV, the Global Alliance for Banking on Values, is detailed in *Nine Visions of Capitalism* Charles Hampden-Turner and Fons Trompenaars Oxford: Infinite Ideas Press, 2015, Chapter 9

121 COULD THE GAMBLING INDUSTRY HELP BUSINESS START-UPS?

The authors cannot blame this idea on anyone else.

122 THE WELFARE CONSORTIUM: HELPING THE POOR TO ORGANIZE

C H-T knows that this idea can work after having lived in and written a book about the Delancey Street Foundation of San Francisco where ex-addicts and ex-convicts run a dozen or so businesses and pay for their own rehabilitation through work. This has now spread to six cities and has been visited by three US Presidents plus Hillary Clinton, see *Sane Asylum: Inside the Delancey Street Foundation.* New York: William Morrow, 1975

123 OVERCOMING THE CRISIS IN PURPOSE

Will Hutton must be one of the very few who made it from journalism to heading an Oxford College. This may have been thanks to his book *The State We Are In* London Jonathan Cape 1996. He was among the first to champion the role of stakeholders and has anticipated many recent events. Especially recommended is *How Good Can We Be?* London Little Brown 2015

124 THE GOD THAT LIMPS

See the book of that title by Norman Colin, World Watch Institute, 1981. The symbolism of Hephaestus is all his. We also much admire Clayton Christensen and his notion of disruptive innovation. But that some technologies do disrupt and have done so in the past does not mean that Facebook's "act fast and break things" is responsible conduct or that hasty expansion using bigots, liars, hostile powers, pornographers and Nazi hate speech to raise the numbers of your customers is an effective way to behave. Claiming that you are a channel of communication not a publisher is disingenuous. Expanding at all costs and monitoring sparingly until others complain is a recipe for disaster. Fierce battles with governments and huge fines are in prospect. Who in their senses wants to contribute to popular hatreds and murdered Muslims? Will the Robber Barons give way to the High Priests of Hate?

125 INVESTING IN SOCIALLY SIGNIFICANT INNOVATION – THE BIG INNOVATION CENTRE AND INTANGIBLE ASSETS

This new innovative thrust could be very important for a number of reasons. First, it has become clear that nations with a purposive industrial strategy agreed among its rulers are developing faster than those who leave it to markets. China is the prime example, but much of the Pacific Rim led the way and the US emerged from World War II expenditures as a super-power among devastated nations. Defence expenditures are largely high tech. The US has the world's largest command economy and military-industrial complex. Second, it is essential that politicians stop their adversarial games and start to think creatively about the future of the nation and its economic development. The cross-party bi-partisanship stimulated by BIC is desperately needed. We must innovate or die, since nearly every mature product can be made cheaper elsewhere and innovation gives us at least a temporary monopoly along with new qualities. Third, the insight that certain technologies are seminal to the future is true and seriously overdue. Historically, the age of canals, steam, manufacturing and mass communications are easy to recognize. We must look for their equivalents today.

126 EXHIBITION OF THE FUTURE

The idea of an Exhibition of the Future with digital moving pictures of the ideas of entrepreneurs, was suggested to C H-T by Tan Teng-Kee, his mature doctoral student, who has recently died but was a professor at Nanyang Technological University in Singapore.

127 NOTES ON BLOCKCHAIN

Most people do not understand Blockchain and many feel vaguely hostile. Its prime example, Bitcoin, seems to excite greed and libertarianism in equal proportions, along with dreams of trashing central banks. I was, however, much taken by Blockchain: The Next Everything by Stephen P Williams, New York: Simon and Schuster, 2019, despite its slightly cynical title. How often have we yearned for a sure-fire technology to save us? But with a strong socio-political input, Blockchain adoption might help a lot. For insights into distributed intelligence and wave theory see Itzhak Bentov Stalking the Wild Pendulum New York: Simon and Schuster, 1980. That the memory area of the brain acts in the manner of a hologram with criss-crossing light-waves, see Karl H Pribram Languages of the Brain Englewood Cliffs: N J. Prentice-Hall 1971. A proximate source at the Big Innovation Centre 20 Victoria Street in London SW1H 0NF who can answer questions is Fernando Santiago at 020 3713 4036 appg-blockchain@biginnovationcentre.com